SYNCHRONICITY

SYNCHRONICITY

C. G. Jung, Psychoanalysis, and Religion

M. D. FABER

Westport, Connecticut
London

Library of Congress Cataloging-in-Publication Data

Faber, M. D. (Mel D.)
    Synchronicity : C. G. Jung, psychoanalysis, and religion / M. D.
Faber.
      p. cm.
    Includes bibliographical references and index.
    ISBN 0–275–96374–8 (alk. paper)
    1. Coincidence. 2. Psychoanalysis and religion. 3. Jung, C. G.
(Carl Gustav), 1875–1961. I. Title.
BF175.5.C65F33   1998
150.19′54—dc21   98–23555

British Library Cataloguing in Publication Data is available.

Library of Congress Catalog Card Number: 98–23555
ISBN: 0–275–96374–8

First published in 1998

Praeger Publishers, 88 Post Road West, Westport, CT 06881
An imprint of Greenwood Publishing Group, Inc.

Printed in the United States of America

The paper used in this book complies with the
Permanent Paper Standard issued by the National
Information Standards Organization (Z39.48–1984).

10 9 8 7 6 5 4 3 2 1

Copyright Acknowledgment

The author and publhlisher gratefully acknowledge permission to reprint extracts from C. G. Jung,
On Synchronicity. Copyright 1977 by Princeton University Press. Reprinted with permission of
Princeton University Press.

For Rebecca and Rebekah,
Paul and Paula,
Ethan,
and Arlene

Contents

Preface

We can understand synchronicity in two basic senses, one "soft," one "hard." Soft synchronicity is simply making a connection between an event and one's existence. I am disposed to phone my ex-wife from whom I have been estranged for several years. The estrangement feels increasingly burdensome and unnatural. One evening as I am dwelling intensively on the issue I duck into a movie. It involves an estranged couple who discover their way toward an amicable, forgiving reconciliation and whose lives are deeply enriched by the emotional breakthrough. I ponder the concurrence of my inward preoccupations and the external event. The book that follows is *not* concerned with soft synchronicity because soft synchronicity is perfectly straightforward. If one is acute, sensitive, intelligent, on the lookout for insights into life and the world, including his own life and his own world, one will be dealing with soft synchronicity on a regular basis in keeping with the motto E.M. Forster placed at the inception of his novel, *Howards End*: only connect. Hard synchronicity is another matter entirely. It derives from the work of C.G. Jung; it raises the discussion to lofty religious and philosophic heights; and it contends the following: remarkable coincidences are not necessarily fortuitous or accidental. The universe, in fact, may be *disposed* to engender hard synchronicities because the universe has a formal or integrative bent which corresponds to, or "touches," the human being's formal or integrative bent. Not only are psyche and matter in contact, they are in *meaningful* contact, the kind that produces *revelations*. Hard synchronicity is my focus in this book.

Much of my discussion, as it turns out, swirls around an actual–and now notorious–synchronistic event that occurred in Jung's consulting room half a century ago. Jung employs the event as a primary example of synchronicity in his writings on the subject. A patient with a Cartesian, rationalistic outlook (Jung presents her as "possessed" by rationalism) arrives for treatment shortly after having dreamed about an Egyptian scarab, or beetle. As she narrates the dream to Jung, a beetle flies into the office. Jung grabs the thing and shows it to the woman who is, of course, flabbergasted. According to Jung, this wondrous event has the effect of breaking down his patient's rationalism and commencing her spiritual rebirth. For Jungians generally, the beetle incident is surrounded by a numinous, otherworldly glow; it is a supreme moment in the history of Jungian psychotherapy and a witness to the accuracy of Jung's synchronistic ruminations. For me, by contrast, the beetle episode is an example of therapeutic manipulation and authoritarianism. It exposes the hidden agenda in both Jungian psychotherapy and Jungian psychological theory. It becomes a battleground on which the problem of synchronicity is thrashed out. To focus the discussion on a central, concrete example of "synchronicity" from the writings of Jung, who invented the term, feels appropriate from the methodological angle.

Let me hasten to say, however, that my purpose in this book is _not_ to refute Jung's theory but to offer an _alternative_ to it. Synchronicity is not something that can be proved or disproved once and for all in a strict, scientific manner. It deals, truth told, with subjective states, and probabilities, and arguments about the ultimate nature of the universe. Jung and his followers may be absolutely correct in their approach to the business. But as I have discovered, synchronicity _can_ be _explained_ in wholly realistic, naturalistic terms. It _can_ be accounted for along psychoanalytic lines which do _not_ oblige us to include _anything_ beyond our own expectable, normative, realistic experience. This is my aim: to remove synchronicity entirely from the world of the paranormal and to place it squarely in the world of naturalistic human behavior. Thus, I will be offering the reader what he can regard as a fresh, original, psychoanalytic approach to synchronicity, a fresh, original psychoanalytic model of synchronistic occurrences. By the time the reader has put the book down, he can ask himself in which direction he wishes to go: toward the realm of Jungian esoterica or toward the realm of psychoanalytic observation.

Why am I doing this? That's easy. Of late Western culture has witnessed what I think of in my own mind as a retreat into magic in an age of science. We are inundated with the "new spirituality," with New Age texts and the pronouncements of New Age gurus, psychic healers, channelers, shamans, neo-pagans, astrologers, and crystal gazers, those who are pushing the supernatural and the paranormal. We have even reached the stage where, for several dollars, one can pick up the telephone and chat with the "psychic" of his choice, with an individual who claims to possess supernatural powers, who claims to be involved, somehow, in an extra-sensorial relationship with the world. Let me not pussyfoot around. I regard Jungian synchronicity, indeed Jungian thought in general, as part of this retreat into magic. I consider it to be regressive, illusory, irrational–a wishful step backwards as opposed to a realistic step forwards. Accordingly, the book that follows is the product of my desire to be on the right side, fighting the good fight. I have no idea, of course, what the outcome will be, but I do know how much better it feels to participate than to look on. I welcome the reader's participation in this book.

1

Jungian Synchronicity:
Questions, Issues, Alternatives

THE AUTHOR'S PURPOSE

I want to offer the reader a psychoanalytic explanation of synchronicity, an explanation to which he can turn as an alternative to the Jungian view. I say "explanation" and "alternative" because synchronistic occurrences as Jung intends them are neither provable nor disprovable in the hard, rigorous sense we traditionally associate with the natural sciences, and with mathematics. The individual who sets out to prove (or disprove) the Jungian theory of synchronicity in a manner similar to that which he would use to prove (or disprove) the heliocentric theory of the solar system or the molecular theory of chemical bonding will simply fall flat on his face. This will emerge clearly as we go, so I won't dwell on it here. It will suffice to say that Jung's notion of synchronicity (and this applies to his followers) is associated inextricably with his notion of archetypes, those elusive, quasi-instinctual entities which Jung employs to explain just about everything that has to do with the dynamics of human psychology. So-called archetypes are the genetically based tendencies which steer or govern our behavior at the unconscious level, including the psychosomatic level, and which characteristically express themselves in powerful, timeless images usually connected to myths, religious rituals, and magic (including alchemy): the gods of antiquity, the pentagram, the mandala, the cross, the wise old man, the great mother, the philosopher's stone. I don't believe it will take the reader very long to recognize the hopelessness of establishing or refuting the correctness of such an idea. One either buys in or one doesn't. Many people do, many people don't.

What this means, among other things of course, is that synchronicity as it is presented by Jung and by his followers, including the gurus of New Age spirituality (James Redfield and Scott Peck, for example), may be absolutely true right down to the last detail and final, paranormal claim. It may *not* be mere chance that my tailor, on the morning of my wife's sudden death, mistakenly sends me a black suit of clothes instead of the blue one I ordered. It may *not* be mere chance that, after dreaming of my old roommate the night before, I run into him at the check-in counter and discover we are *both* flying to Honolulu, at 8:15 AM. The physical world *may* be infused with "psyche" or "spirit" or some such. The physical world *may* possess a kind of subtle "intelligence" with emergent, formal tendencies and teleological intentions which touch and engage my subjective human purposes, however trivial and idiosyncratic they appear to be. Higher, supernatural forces *may* be watching over me, prodding me in the right direction, helping me to make the right choices, to avoid the pitfalls (this above all is the claim of Jungian synchronicity). Mind *may* be able to influence matter, even at a distance: praying for the remission of cancer in Boston may aid someone dying of it in Toronto. Fantasying about an earthquake a few hours before its occurrence may somehow be involved in its occurrence. Let me hasten to say that I do not believe any of this, personally. Indeed, I regard such ideas as more or less regressive and wishful (I will get to the "more or less" eventually, I promise). I also don't like to think of such ideas finding a legitimate place in the Western culture in which I live and about which I care. I don't like to think of my social, intellectual world slipping and sliding toward mumbo jumbo and superstition and credulity. At the same time, I recognize that people *come* to the notion of synchronicity, and buy in to it and cling on to it, for compelling emotional reasons–and not merely synchronicity but the mystical, religious system that Jung and his followers push and pass off as psychology. There are human *needs* here, adaptive strategies with possible evolutionary significance, cunning unconscious responses to the very real problems that plague us: anomie, alienation, loneliness, divorce, unemployment, over-crowding, senseless violence, pollution, and crime, not to mention the old existential givens of separation, loss, and death all of which for many harbor primal terror. Synchronicity has enormous, widespread appeal today (it is becoming a household word) because it speaks positively to people who feel powerless and alone. I want to get at this here. I want to comprehend it, fully. I want to look at synchronicity's attractiveness in a way that may allow us to understand ourselves and our problems a little better than we presently do. I have no intention of announcing as one might do in an article in a skeptical magazine that synchronicity is simply bunk and should be tossed in the ash can of supernatural absurdities. Synchronicity *is* largely bunk, but it is bunk that has a genuine human face and a genuine human meaning. It is bunk that sheds light on crucial psychological, biological, sociological, and religious issues. It is bunk that we can and should *use*, as curious and concerned inhabitants of the planet. Jung was a passionate, gifted thinker committed to knowledge and fearless in his pursuit of the truth. What he has to say is, from my perspective, often mistaken (and often badly written), but it is also inspirational. After all, it inspired this book.

Permit me to expand a little on my purpose as I have just set it out in the previous paragraphs. I plan to explore synchronicity along psychoanalytic lines in a way that will bring it over entirely to the realm of naturalistic events. Naturalism is defined as a theory denying that an event or object has a supernatural significance. I will do away with archetype, with spirit, with soul, with psyche imploding into matter, and with the fringy application of quantum theory–used these days to justify any and all metaphysical notions to which one feels an attachment (matter is really energy and spirit is really energy; because energy is of a piece and can't be separated, we are all joined together in a spiritual cosmos). The kind of procedure I am about to launch is often called "unpacking," or "deconstructing," or "demystifying," all of which expressions go very well indeed to the heart of my intention. Yet I must also reemphasize the *constructive* side of this book, its attempt to afford us a broad, far-reaching insight into our essential human characters, our essential human natures, by developing a detailed, full-fledged psychoanalytic account of synchronicity, one that can be used as a balance to the Jungian outlook. Because synchronicity is at the center of Jung's religious-psychological edifice, because in the words of an expert it is "the single theory with the most far-reaching implications for Jung's psychology" (Aziz 1990, 1), the deconstruction or demystification or unpacking that follows will bear crucially on the whole of Jung's thought. And most assuredly, this is one of my related purposes: to demonstrate, in a preliminary way at least, the extent to which all of Jung's work can be stripped of its spiritual implications, brought smoothly and comfortably into a naturalistic framework, made easily intelligible along psychoanalytic lines which lead ultimately to normative behaviors, empirical, observational, developmental behaviors, even to some degree testable behaviors, none of which require explanation that is not rooted firmly in naturalistic ground.

PSYCHOANALYSIS AFTER FREUD

The psychoanalytic direction from which I will be approaching synchronicity is ultimately indebted to Freud, but it is indebted directly and overwhelmingly to several of his followers whose work becomes prominent in the decades following Freud's death. Hence, I will *not* be relying here on the Oedipus complex, sexuality, the "discharge" of aggressive and libidinal "drives," the primary role of the father in emotional life, the wish-fulfillment theory of dreams, or the phylogenetic unconscious (Mr. Hyde of Jekyll and Hyde fame) as it is inherited from our primitive, Darwinian past. I will rely instead upon the work of 1) Melanie Klein, with its emphasis on the child's tendency to *internalize* the environment, to create a world of *internalized objects*, or presences, from which arise a number of early, primal fantasies as well as a number of early, primal defenses most notably projective identification and splitting the residues of which are frequently found in the emotional and intellectual lives of adults; 2) the work of Ronald Fairbairn, with its powerful insistence (supported by vivid clinical case studies) that newcomers to this world do not seek primarily to release their "instinctual energies" but to *find and connect with the caregiver*, the object upon whom their physical and emotional well-being depends. Put simply, the baby seeks the breast as opposed to a "reduction of tension"; 3) the work of Donald Winnicott, with its seminal notions of a) good-enough mothering, the foundation of normal cognitive and emotional life; b) transitional objects (blankets, teddy bears, story books), those substitutive items to which the child turns as he copes with separation from the caregiver (disillusionment); c) potential space, the inner, psychological realm where the child learns to fashion a reality from the creative capacities of his own mind as they interact with the external environment. This primary, persistent *illusion* (the aftermath of disillusionment) comprises a synthesizing, epistemological complement to our traditional notions of subjective and objective. Reality, holds Winnicott, is always both inner and outer *simultaneously*, is always a mix; 4) the work of John Bowlby and his followers (Mary Ainsworth, Robert Karen) which underscores the decisive role of attachment and loss in our maturational growth. For Bowlby, soothing, secure attachment to an available caregiving figure is the *sine qua non* of satisfactory human development, and early separation (either actual, physical separation or the kind of separation that is fostered by an ambivalent or rejecting parent) is the root cause of human malaise. Bowlby's lifelong aim was to put psychoanalysis squarely on an empirical footing; 5) the work of Margaret Mahler and associates where the issues of separation and attachment are explored in close connection with the child's biological and emotional need to *differentiate* himself/herself from the caretaker and gain a stable, separate identity. For Mahler, the struggle between separation and attachment, or differentiation and merger, is the elemental struggle of our being. Even as we manage to differentiate ourselves from the maternal presence we are devising, often unconsciously, a number of strategies for re-merging with that presence at the mental-emotional level. The struggle between separation and union, says Mahler, ends only when we die; 6) the detailed, observational work of Daniel Stern which concentrates upon a) the emotional and perceptual interactions of the early, dyadic relationship; b) the parent's attempt to *attune* herself to her child; c) the mutual delight of parent and child who act *in synch* with one another (here we touch explicitly and for the first time on the tie between synchronicity and modern psychoanalysis); d) the gradual creation of the newcomer's inner world where the caregiver's loving ministrations, internalized by the growing child, become the source of the inward companionship that most of us are able to experience when we are alone. The self as Stern conceives of it is based upon internalizations of the *other*; this gives us our wonderful capacity to sense the other's presence within even when the other is absent (in psychoanalytic circles this is called "dual-unity"); 7) the work of Christopher Bollas where we come to appreciate the *transformational* role of the caregiver in the child's early years. Again and again the parent *transforms* the child's actual world, changing discomfort into pleasure, or relief: hunger into satiety, anxiety into security, wetness into dryness, and so forth. Bollas helps us to realize that a search for transformation in later life is often rooted unconsciously in a search for the original transformational object of childhood; 8) the work of Stephen Mitchell, with its emphasis upon the primary role of *relations* in human experience. For Mitchell, we are social to the root, and all our behaviors, whether in the spheres of work, play, family, worship, or intimacy, harbor some aspect of *relationship*, of human *interaction*, both at their primal, foundational source in the past and their more immediate, desire-driven source in the present. What each of these thinkers has in common with the rest in perhaps best expressed in Fairbairn's key notion, at the bedrock of present-day psychoanalysis, that the child seeks the object, the person, the relation, and not the discharge of his oral or anal instincts. Moving away from its early conceptualizations, from its close connection to the physical sciences of the nineteenth century, psychoanalysis has become a person-centered, relation-centered psychology, a psychology of object-relations, preoccupied primarily with the ways in which people interact with one another, and with the fantasies, or the projections, that invariably arise from those interactions.

I believe this overview underscores the extent to which modern psychoanalysis strives to approach human behavior from an empirical perspective, strives to avoid obtaining its data primarily from the ruminations of its theorists, strives in short to give clinical, observational studies a place of honor at the head of the table. Bowlby, Winnicott, Mahler, Stern: they *look* at children long and hard, and they fashion their analytic positions directly out of that looking. They do not come to children bearing axiomatic presuppositions (archetypes, for example) along with them. I am not suggesting that present-day psychoanalysts *never* employ inferential material as they go about their business, never take data from the analyses of adults and, in the light of that data, characterize the early interpersonal world of those very adults. Of course this occurs; indeed, it occurs *of necessity*. We can not climb into time-machines with our patients and travel backwards. We *must* in many instances "interpret" or "read" ourselves into the past, for if we let the past go we let the foundation go; we let the possible determinants of behavior go; we let one rich source of our insight go. Perhaps the major item on which the vast majority of psychoanalysts, psychiatrists, and psychotherapists agree these days is the all important role of the past–and that usually means the deep, familial past–in shaping the conduct of grown-ups in the present (see Horgan 1996, 106). Yet increasingly in modern psychoanalysis inferential interpretation is influenced, even governed by, conclusions drawn from ongoing clinical research; increasingly the theorizers are the clinicians and the clinicians the theorizers. We will never, obviously, have perfect objectivity here, if there is such a thing. To study human beings, or better, to have certain human beings studying other human beings will never lead to the kind of certitude that arises when certain human beings study, say, table salt. But we can try. In a cautious, responsible, healthily skeptical frame of mind we can try to be as objective as possible, try to discern what is there, actually there, try to make our analytical narratives jibe with what we believe to be the givens of human interaction during life's early stages, and later stages too, bearing in mind always that culture and hence experience are ceaselessly changing, even as we probe them. After all, what choice *have* we? Should we stop exploring the early period because we can't be perfectly objective about it? Should we return to the Middle Ages when the study of infants and children was non-existent? Should we do for little monkeys and little rats what we won't do for ourselves? Or should we do the best we can, and in a flexible, dialectical spirit bring our insight to our fellow creatures (both sick and well) who doubtless wish to enjoy all the knowledge they can gain, of both themselves and others? In my view, there is only one way to answer these questions. But let's get more specific, now, about what it is exactly that we'll be unpacking in subsequent sections.

SYNCHRONICITY, ARCHETYPE, *UNUS MUNDUS*, AND *IMAGO DEI*

Jungian synchronicity has two chief components, or sides, neither of which can be separated from the other as I am about to separate them here for the sake of our discussion. First, there is the physical side of the business, the bare facts of the coincidence, the items or objects that come into a remarkable, improbable relationship in the so-called external world: my dream of an exotic, rarely seen bird and my glimpse of an identical creature in the treetops the very next day; my sudden, inexplicable interest in paganism and the arrival in the mail of a book on the subject only hours after my interest peaks. We might call this the *matter* side of the *unus mundus*–the *one world* of matter and psyche from which reality ultimately arises. Secondly, we have the affective or emotional side of the event, the side that not only registers the coincidence but perceives its uncanny, powerful nature, its prophetic quality, its store of meaning, its connection to the struggles and searchings of one's own life. For Jung and his followers this is the creative side of synchronicity, the side that obtains from the synchronous event the kind of knowledge one might gain upon witnessing a marvel or a miracle. In this way, Jung's theory of synchronicity is in considerable measure a theory of psychological *response*. The question arises immediately, of course, whence comes this response? What exactly is its psychological origin? From a Jungian angle the answer is perfectly clear: the powerful emotion triggered by synchronicity comes directly from the collective unconscious, from the archetypal world, from the stock or store of quasi-instinctual tendencies and images that each of us has been carrying around since birth, and perhaps even *before* birth, to the extent that each of us brings with him to this world what we can call an immortal soul. Our response, in short, is phylogenetic rather than ontogenetic; it is rooted in our inherited inclinations as opposed to our personal experiences.

Yet there is more. The moment of synchronicity is *numinous*. The emotions that spring forth therein do not arise from the archetypal world in some diffuse, general way; on the contrary, they arise specifically from an engagement of the *religious archetype*, one's deep, instinctual awareness of godhead, the *imago Dei* that governs our spiritual or religious nature and that triggers our affective response when we confront the miraculous, the mysterious, the divine. In the synchronous moment we show an exquisite sensitivity to nature's harmonious plan, to the *a priori* realm of timeless form where everything (both mental and physical) is connected to everything else–once again, the *unus mundus* of spiritual apprehension. Yet there is more still: the religious archetype is, for Jung and his followers, the archetype of the *self*, the archetype of our integrated, ordered identity, or being, the archetype of our intimate relation to the harmonious nature in which we discover ourselves and of which we comprise an inseparable part. In a word, *we* are divine; *we* harbor divinity within; *we* are godhead, all of which truths are expressed externally through religious symbols, the pentagram for example, where the *imago Dei* and the *unus mundus* are aesthetically framed by the human creature within whom divine harmonies flow. All too often in our actual experience, maintain Jungians, we are cut off from this archetype, alienated from our divine, harmonious nature ("the world is too much with us"), and it is the job of the Jungian therapist precisely to guide us toward a happy reunion, where we may rest whole.

Note how the matter of our origins goes in the literature; I could cite a hundred examples but three or four will do. Jung writes in a letter (July 29, 1939) to a psychotherapist,

> originally we were all born out of a world of wholeness and in the first years of life are still completely contained in it. There we have all knowledge without knowing it. Later we lose it, and call it progress when we remember it again.

According to the famous Jungian analyst Edward Edinger (1972, 10) who feels inclined to quote Wordsworth on this score, we come to the world "Not in entire forgetfulness, / And not in utter nakedness, / But trailing clouds of glory . . . / From God who is our home." Childhood, says Edinger (ibid), is "near to deity." For June Singer (1972, 108), also a famous Jungian analyst who is drawn to poetry, Tennyson hits the nail on the head in *De Profundis* when he metaphorically maintains that children come to the planet, "out of the deep, . . . / Out of the deep." Singer chooses to gloss "the deep" as "the primordial past of humanity." It probably had something to do in Tennyson with the Gnostic idea of Pleroma, but that doesn't really matter very much here. What we must note above all is the *distance* between views such as these and the views of modern psychoanalysis where our "origins" reside not in "clouds of glory" or "the deep" but in the real give-and-take of the real interactions that occur between the real parent and child during the real early period of our lives. What we bring to the world is a wide variety of genetic traits and potentials; that's all. What *happens* to these traits and potentials is a matter of *relations with others*, relations that are eventually internalized by the growing child to become the scaffolding of his/her subsequent character. Far from being "contained" in a "world of wholeness," a typical idealization of childhood on Jung's part (see Charet 1993, 63), newcomers to this earth find themselves coping with the imperfections (and sometimes dysfunctions) of their environment, responding to their frustrations and troubles with powerful and persistent psychological defenses such as splitting and projection, and emerging from the early time either more or less prepared by good-enough mothering for the inescapable struggles to come, or scathed badly enough to require some special attention. Fortunately, most of us manage to make it through to old-fashioned, problematical normalcy.

The gulf that divides the Jungian view from the view of current psychoanalysis is perhaps best captured in a couple of sentences by Jean Houston (1996, 132) in which we are told "to begin by placing our roots in heaven, in the realm of creation and archetypal patterns. Then we examine our lives to discover the pattern and its face, not only in childhood but throughout our lives." In other words, *look away*, look up, look to heaven as opposed to earth; do not observe what is actually occurring between people in the actual world as you commence your investigations of human origins, human behavior, human psychology; rather, impose "archetypal patterns" on your material; let "archetypal patterns" govern your studies, not the interpersonal life that is going on in front of your nose. Houston's way of expressing things may appear to be extreme, but it is in reality an accurate reflection of the mainstream Jungian a· proach. And no wonder, for as Charet (1993, 63, 83) observes in his fine historical study, *Spiritualism and the Foundation of C.G. Jung's Psychology* to which I referred the reader a moment earlier,

> there is ample evidence that Jung did not explore the life of childhood in order to establish the precise causes of la.er psychiatric and psychological disorders . . . The bulk of Jung's writings are concerned with elucidating the archetypal background against which the experience of adult life should be understood . . . Jung idealized children . . . [His] psychology has largely ignored childhood.

Anthony Storr (1973, 66) puts it this way in *C.G. Jung*: "there is very little indeed to be found specifically upon the psychology of children throughout the *Collected Works* of Jung." Thus when present-day Jungians advise us to *look away* from the child's interpersonal world in establishing our psychological origins, when they advise us to look, of all places, to "heaven," they are only echoing the views of their master.

Our task is beginning to emerge in earnest: to unpack the notion of synchronicity is not merely to unpack the notion of archetypes, including of course the archetype of religion; it is also to determine along observational, clinical lines the psychodynamic source of the emotion, the affect, the *response* that for Jung and his followers is the absolute prerequisite for the occurrence of synchronicity in the first place. Without the emotion, without the affect, without a psychological response that goes back to our very origins as people (our inherited archetypal tendencies), we just have a coincidence, an odd, memorable juxtaposition of disparate events that does not ultimately mean anything. Because Jung's theory of response in grounded in phylogeny, in an archetypal world that somehow resides behind or beneath our reactions to things, there is no way to put that theory to the test, to see the extent to which it jibes or fails to jibe with the results of our close, painstaking, observational studies of children during the early period. Moreover, to derive our explanation of synchronicity–and by that I mean our explanation of its emotional significance–from clinical, observational materials is to render the archetypal theory otiose, superfluous, unnecessary. If we can explain synchronicity, really explain it in a logical, coherent, consistent, convincing, clinical way that does not require the presence of unseen, assumptive, phylogenetic factors, then we had better set those factors aside. In short, we had better give Jung and his followers a shave with Occam's razor and be done with it. After all, what is the alternative? Are we to discover by looking and seeing the factors that inform our early experience and that enter later into the synchronous moment, and then cry, "Hold it! There is more here than meets the eye! Archetypes are at work. Don't flatter yourself to think your empirical psychology can explain all this!" Why would anyone *want* to take this line? We don't have to struggle very long to find the answer: one wants to take this line because one wants our human origins to derive from something other than, something greater than, our mere human psychological and biological interactions; one wants to take this line because one wants to tender something mighty, something grand, something irresistible as a final precipitating agent; one wants to take this line because one wants to connect and to subordinate our ordinary, earthly purposes to a realm that contains them, transfigures them, transcends them. The archetype of *religion* is coming into view.

PHYLOGENETIC RELIGION AT CENTER STAGE

Let's note the manner in which, over the years, the archetype of religion emerges from Jung's work. In an early paper, "The Father in the

Destiny of the Individual" (FP, 321),[1] composed when he was still under Freud's influence, Jung approximates what we might call today an object-relations perspective, writing,

> the parental influence, dating from the early infantile period, is repressed and sinks into the unconscious, but it is not eliminated; by invisible threads it directs the apparently individual workings of the maturing mind. Like everything that has fallen into the unconscious, the infantile situation still sends up dim, premonitory feelings, feelings of being secretly guided by otherworldly influences. Normally these feelings are not referred back to the father, but to a positive or negative deity.

Storr (1973, 42) remarks on this passage:

> Jung appears to consider that the archetypal images take origin from infantile experience, rather than being based upon inherited predispositions. If Jung had continued to maintain this point of view about the origin of archetypal images, he would have gained wider acceptance for his psychology.

This strikes me as an accurate evaluation. Of particular interest, however, is that Jung's outlook comes close to the view of *synchronicity* we will be developing in later sections: the infantile unconscious sends up feelings of being "secretly guided" by "otherworldly influences," feelings that are originally personal and subsequently projected onto a "deity." Jung was fascinated by synchronicity throughout the course of his adult life, and certainly by the time he joined Freud's Viennese group. Do we have a simple, embryonic view of synchronicity here, subsequently to be modified along archetypal lines? Perhaps. Although Jung's idea of secret guidance by otherworldly influence requires meticulous amplification based upon observational studies before it can be offered as an alternative to his mature theory, it is remarkably close to the spiritual interpretation of coincidence discovered in the present-day Jungian literature. We can keep this in mind as we go.

Here is a second passage, this time from *Symbols of Transformation* (ST, 89) which was composed when Jung was breaking away from Freud in earnest:

> the regressive reactivation of the father and mother imagos plays an important role in religion. The benefits of religion are equivalent, in their effects, to the parental care lavished upon the child, and religious feelings are rooted in unconscious memories of certain tender emotions in

early infancy–memories of archetypal intuitions, as expressed in the
[Egyptian] hymn: 'I am in my country, I come into my city. I am daily
together with my father, Atum.' . . . In God we honor the energy of the
archetype.

The origin of religious feeling is still rooted in unconscious memories of
infancy; now, however, these memories themselves are of "archetypal
intuitions." They do not derive immediately from the interpersonal world
of parent and child but from something phylogenetic, something that is
somehow inherited, given, innate. Needless to say, there is no way for
Jung to support this directly, to explain to us how "adult memories" of
"early infancy" can be in actuality "adult memories" of "archetypal
intuitions." As everyone knows, Jung *tries* to support this by reminding us
that certain timeless images, of the great mother for example, appear all
over the world and look very much alike. Yet there is no reason to believe
that such images do not arise individually, ontogenetically, personally as it
were, by virtue of the fact that mothering and childhood are very much
alike all over the world. Ontogenetic explanations of ubiquitous symbols
are just as convincing as phylogenetic ones, and because ontogenetic
explanations are simpler, that is, because they are derived directly from
what is *there*, we have no good reason to account for ubiquitous symbols
by alluding to items that are, and must remain, unseen (archetypes).

Here is a third and final passage, from *Archetypes of the Collective
Unconscious* (ACU, 62-3), written during the 1930's when Jung's psychology was achieving its full, mature expression:

the psychologist knows how much religious ideas have to do with parental imagos. History has preserved overwhelming evidence of this,
quite apart from modern medical findings, which have led certain people to suppose that the relationship to the parents is the real origin of religious ideas. This hypothesis is based upon very poor knowledge of the
facts . . . The only thing we know positively from psychological experience is that theistic ideas are associated with the parental imagos, and
that our patients are mostly unconscious of them. If the corresponding
projections cannot be withdrawn through insight, then we have every
reason to suspect the presence of emotional contents of a religious nature . . . So far as we have any information about man, we know that he
has always and everywhere been under the influence of dominating
ideas . . . A man without a dominating *representation collective* would
be a thoroughly abnormal phenomenon. But such a person exists only in
the fantasies of isolated individuals who are deluded about themselves.
They are mistaken not only about the existence of religious ideas, but
also and especially about their intensity.

Jung then asserts (ACU, 63),

> the archetype behind a religious idea has, like every instinct, its specific energy, which it does not lose even if the conscious mind ignores it. Just as it can be assumed . . . that every man possesses all the average human functions and qualities, so we may expect the presence of normal religious factors, the archetypes, and this expectation does not prove fallacious. Anyone who succeeds in putting off the mantle of faith can do so only because another lies close to hand. No one can escape the prejudice of being human.

What a shift from the early materials in Jung's essay on the father! Jung is now suggesting that patients who *won't let go* of their "theistic" projections, who hang on to them despite the "insight" afforded by analytical psychology, must be under the influence of something more basic, more tenacious, more unyielding than the mere personal unconscious, namely the archetypes of the collective unconscious, and in particular the archetype of religion, the "normal religious factor." I can not see *any* logic in this at all, but there it is–a *non sequitur* if there ever was one. Surely patients hang on to their projections for a wide variety of reasons, reasons which do *not* require phylogenetic explanations. Moreover, says Jung, if anyone does succeed in putting off the "mantle of faith," that is, if anyone does succeed in withdrawing his projections from a specific "theism," it is only because he has found another one to take its place. To be religious is now equated with being human, and being human is now equated with having an addiction to religious behaviors.

Accordingly, our unpacking of synchronicity will necessitate our unpacking of *all this*, for as we have seen, synchronicity in Jung exists only when the archetype of religion is at work. We must ask, from a purely ontogenetic angle or the angle of the personal unconscious, *why* do people hang on so persistently to their "theistic" projections? *Why* do they refuse to let them go? And *why*, if they succeed through "insight" in dropping a particular religious involvement, do they head straight for another one? What makes the tie to religion so important, so vital, so addictive, so human? With reference to synchronicity in particular, *why* do people insist that coincidental events speak for a supernatural presence in their lives? *Why* do they crave a connection to a higher, directive, encompassing spiritual power? Because *we* are not permitted, like Jung, to offer archetypal solutions to such problems, because *we* must rely only upon what is demonstrably there, *we* are obliged to take the religious urge apart, to break it down into its psychological components, to see it as an acting-out of elemental wishes and needs rooted in the actual experience of the early period. Religious archetype for us is but a *name* for a constellation of individual, personal, largely unconscious items which are themselves the composites of religious archetype. The trail of synchronicity may lead us to the hidden wellsprings of Jung's religious psychology as a whole.

SYNCHRONICITY IN THE CONSULTING ROOM

The most famous and influential example of synchronicity in Jung originates in Jung's consulting room as he interacts with one of his patients. What this means psychoanalytically should be obvious enough: the most famous synchronous moment in Jung springs immediately from a *transference relationship*, the *kind* of relationship during the course of which the patient *regresses* to earlier stages of psychosexual development and *transfers* to the doctor a constellation of feelings which ultimately reflect the original tie to the parent. It is from precisely this direction, the direction of the consulting room, that vital clues to the underlying psychological nature of synchronicity may emerge. Here is the famous example from Jung's essay, *On Synchronicity: An Acausal Connecting Principle* (S, 437-39): "a young woman I was treating had, at a critical moment, a dream in which she was given a golden scarab. While she was telling me this dream I sat with my back to the closed window. Suddenly I heard a noise behind me, like a gentle tapping. I turned round and saw a flying insect knocking against the window-pane from outside. I opened the window and caught the creature in the air as it flew in. It was the nearest analogy to a Golden Scarab that one finds in our latitudes, a scarabaeid beetle, the common rose-chafer." Jung goes on,

> There . . . seems to be an archetypal foundation to the . . . case. It was an extraordinarily difficult case to treat, and up to the time of the dream little or no progress had been made . . . I should explain that the main reason for this was my patient's animus, which was steeped in Cartesian philosophy and clung so rigidly to its own idea of reality that the efforts of three doctors . . . had not been able to weaken it. Evidently something quite irrational was needed which was beyond my powers to produce. The dream alone was enough to disturb ever so slightly the rationalistic attitude of my patient. But when the 'scarab' came flying in through the window in actual fact, her natural being could burst through the armor of her animus possession and the process of transformation could at last begin to move. Any essential change of attitude signifies psychic renewal which is usually accompanied by symbols of rebirth in the patient's dreams and fantasies. The scarab is a classic example of a rebirth symbol.

And so the passage ends.

Fully to unpack synchronicity, then, is to demonstrate the manner in which the synchronous moment calls into play *the ground of the transference*, the period in which the child perceives the parent as all-powerful, all-knowing, magical, numinous. We've already seen that synchronicity involves an awakening of the religious archetype, as is apparently the case in the beetle episode just cited. We may now suspect that the religious archetype has something to do with the kind of emotion that emerges in the transference encounter. What Jung fails to explore or even to mention in his famous instance of synchronicity is *his own role* in triggering and enhancing the uncanny, numinous effect of the insect's entrance. To believe that powerful forces are guiding one's existence in mysterious ways may very well be to project upon the universe a version of one's own life as it originally *was* in the infantile situation and as it currently *is* in the transference to the doctor, the person toward whom one *regresses emotionally* as the treatment goes along. The first authority is the parent; the finally authority is the deity: somewhere in-between stands the Jungian analyst whose job is to guide the patient to the archetypal world.

ANCIENT ORACLES, MODERN ORACLES

Jung was powerfully drawn to the *I Ching*, an ancient oracular Chinese text that comprises on the one hand an instrument of divination (the practice of foretelling events or of discovering secret knowledge by supernatural means) and on the other a compendium of philosophical insights. One throws coins or counts sticks and is thereby directed to the portion of the book that ostensibly bears on one's personal concerns. Feibleman (1976, 119) in a study of Oriental thought remarks,

> throughout Chinese history the *I Ching* continued an old tradition which included magic and spirits exercising supernatural powers. The spirits departed early, however, and with them the supernatural, after meeting the opposition of Confucius and his followers. What was left, and what continues still to be practiced, is what may be called earthbound divination . . . The *I Ching* no longer promises to control the future but only to predict it; therein lies its durability.

As for the *kind* of oracular pronouncement one discovers in this marvelous old tome (the world's huge, original fortune cookie), it might be "a dragon lies hid and there should be no expenditure," or "fullness cannot endure for long," or "above wood there is fire," and so forth (see Hughes 1971, 9-10).

The *I Ching* interested Jung because it was based on psychological projection, on the participant's capacity to find in a specific passage a link to his own idiosyncratic preoccupations. It was not mere *chance* that made the book work; it was the user's creative ability, his flare for reading his own personal agenda into the cryptic message. Here was an obvious link to synchronicity: a coincidence, an accident, brings to the surface a connection one could not quite see on his own. Jung called this is his *Foreword to the 'I Ching'* (F, 192) the "interdependence of objective events" with the "subjective (psychic) states of the observer." Yet there is an additional point to be made, the main point in fact, which ties the *I Ching* not only to synchronicity in general but to the *kind* of synchronicity we just witnessed in Jung's office.

Just as the therapist's *authoritative* relationship to the patient may trigger and enhance the "archetypal" meaning of a coincidence brought forward in the consulting room, just as the therapist's transferential *hold* on the patient may work the transformational miracle, so may the hallowed, oracular, authoritative nature of the *I Ching* have its effect on the participant who is throwing the coins or counting the sticks. Writes Hellmut Wilhelm (1973, 9),

> [the *I Ching*] was not a human medium that was consulted but a collection of texts whose authority and value the oracle seeker accepted unquestioningly. For these texts represented to him a fully rounded system, an ordered framework, within which a point to be established would give his momentary situation and what it implied. This system was created by men of ancient times, whom the questioner revered as custodians of a wisdom full of awareness of the connection between what is decreed and what happens. It was from them that he drew his information.

The Chinese landlord, or farmer, or prince throws the coins and then listens *in awe*, listens to the *oracle,* to the magical, powerful *authority* from which he gets his direction, his "tip." Can it all be mere chance? To turn the matter again toward Jung's consulting room, it is the *analyst* who is full of awareness; it is the analyst who is the custodian of wisdom; it is the analyst who represents an ordered framework, a rounded system to which the needy, dependent patient aspires. The oracular nature of the *I Ching* is mirrored in the analyst's oracular nature, the analyst who today represents *our* avenue to hidden knowledge and sudden enlightenment. The patient tells Jung her dream about a beetle and, lo and behold, Jung holds out a beetle in his hand! What a wondrous event! What patient could resist, could argue, could say, for example, "rose-chafers are quite common in Switzerland at this time of the year; we surely do have a coincidence here, but that's all." I have the feeling that Dr. Jung's presence in the room made *that* sort of interpretation unlikely. This, then, is the *I Ching's* connection to synchronicity: both may rely upon psychological regression to a time when higher powers (parents) could miraculously discover and respond to one's needs, to a time when the universe *did* have the capacity to espy one's requirements in a mysterious, inexplicable way. One can *project* into the oracle or the analyst the same omnipotence, the same omniscience, the same all-powerful qualities that one experienced during the early period when "objective events" (parental ministrations) *were* connected "psychically" to one's wishes and fears. It is in this particular, peculiar manner that both the *I Ching* and synchronicity may assume the parent's place.

SYNCHRONICITY IN THE NEW AGE

Synchronicity has gone pop. Since the time of Jung's original formulations in the early 1950's, the idea has taken on a life of its own to become in our own day a major spiritual item, a major spiritual entity as it were. Synchronicity is now "a household word" (Mansfield 1995, 22), as I mentioned in an earlier section. Not only do we have large numbers of people experiencing synchronous events on a regular basis, we even have a rock group, The Police, choosing to give one of their albums the groovy title: *Synchronicity* climbed to the top of the charts in very brisk fashion indeed. Wendy Kaminer (1996) gets at the contagion effectively in her scathing article, *The Latest Fashion in Irrationality*. The article is, in its opening sections, an analysis-review of James Redfield's (1993) *The Celestine Prophecy*, itself a New Age classic with ten million copies in print and with synchronicity as one of its central concerns. Kaminer (104) writes,

> like virtually all books of its genre, *The Celestine Prophecy* can confidently demand that readers suspend their disbelief because it tells so many people precisely what they want to hear. Its message is that there is no such thing as a coincidence; there are no chance encounters, no arbitrary events, no reasons for existential angst. There is only cosmic synchronicity, to which we become attuned as we evolve spiritually. (The assurance that events are not random, that we live in a universe ordered by a benign supernatural being, is repeated in many popular spirituality books.)

One of those "popular spirituality books," as it turns out, is Scott Peck's

(1988) *The Road Less Traveled*, another New Age classic with five million copies sold, and a curious combination of Protestant sermonizing and Jungian theorizing, including of course Jung's concept of synchronicity. Asserting in a classic Jungian moment guaranteed to drive more orthodox Christian theologians wild that "our unconscious is God," the "God within," Peck (259, 281) speaks of synchronicity as a "miracle of Grace," as evidence of God's loving interventions in our lives. Synchronicity, Peck (312) suggests, diminishes the "sense of aloneness" that many of us feel on "the spiritual journey," on "the less traveled road of spiritual growth." It would be hard to miss the accent of the New Age here. Colin Wilson (1984, 116) sums things up nicely for us in his excellent volume, *C.G. Jung: Lord of the Underworld*: synchronicity "may be understood . . . as a kind of nudge from some unknown guardian angel, whose purpose is to tell us that life is not as meaningless as it looks." This brings me to the point.

I am as much concerned with synchronicity's current usage and meaning as I am concerned with Jung's original essay and its implications for Jung's psychology as a whole. I want to explore synchronicity as a kind of spiritual fad, a lively, influential New Age idea that is increasingly attractive to New Age savants, to our present-day experts in the supernatural, the spiritual universe, the province of soul, the transcendent realm, and all the endless rest of it. This means I will be employing psychoanalysis in an old-fashioned way which stems from its revolutionary origins in Europe at the turn of the century, namely as a method of *cultural critique*, a method of unpacking, of demystifying, major and minor cultural institutions in the spheres of politics, economics, and religion. To put it somewhat differently, I want to say why, from the psychoanalytic angle, people today feel inclined to spy an angel on their shoulder, to give a supernatural, synchronistic meaning to the title of that Gershwin tune, *Someone To Watch Over Me*. Kaminer and Wilson do a good job in putting their finger on synchronicity's essence in a general way; our job here will be to pin the matter down more specifically in critical psychoanalytic terms. Perhaps in doing this we will see how accurate a version of Jung's original idea, with its complexities of archetypes and modern physics, the popular idea actually is. Does the Jungian theory, including its amplification in the hands of the Jungian specialists, boil down to the simple conviction that someone is *there*, that we are not *alone*, that a Big One is looking out for us little ones? Or is the popular view a childish distortion of Dr. Jung's conceptualizations?

COINCIDENCE

Let's turn now to the issue of coincidence, the objective or material side of synchronicity, as Jung might say. How are we to understand the concurrence of discrete, highly improbabilistic events like the ones I briefly described in the context: my dream of a rare, exotic bird and my discovery of an identical creature in the treetops the very next day, or a putative error on the tailor's part which finds me, an hour after my wife's sudden death, staring at a black suit of clothes instead of the blue one I ordered? Are straightforward, materialistic, rational explanations sufficient to account for such things? Does the appearance of Jung's notorious beetle defy our comprehension, in the usual sense of the term? True, Jung's theory is ultimately a theory of emotional response: the archetype must be "constellated" for synchronicity to occur. Yet it is *coincidence* that goads the archetype; it is coincidence that arouses the collective unconscious and permits the individual to profit from its ancient store of wisdom.

What we must bear in mind above all about coincidence, Peter Watson (1981) informs us in his definitive treatment of the subject, is that rare events, even remarkably rare events, do in fact occur, all around us, all the time, and for no discernible higher, or spiritual, purpose. "I cannot stress too much," writes Watson (135), "that rare events do happen. People do die in airplane crashes and get struck by lightning–they even make killings on the tables at Monte Carlo and Las Vegas." Watson goes on to describe a remarkable event that took place in 1976 aboard the liner *Queen Elizabeth II* during a crossing from Southhampton to New York. A young English gentleman tumbled overboard while intoxicated and tossed about in the Atlantic for half an hour before his absence was noted by his friends. The captain wheeled the ship around and followed the traces of its wake. "Astounding as it may seem," Watson informs us (135), "the Englishman was found thrashing about in the water, his champagne glass still in his hand." Watson concludes by observing that the "odds against finding someone in an ocean swell like that must be enormous–but it happened."

Once again, this time with the spiritual dimension implicitly in view: "improbable events *do* occur without the need to assume anything supernatural to account for them" (Watson 1981, 132). The odds that you will be dealt a royal flush during your next hand of poker, notes Watson (105), are 1 in 649,740; these are enormous odds, yet people on occasion are dealt a royal flush. The odds that you will die during the course of a surgical operation are 1 in 40,000; these are still extremely high odds, yet people do die in surgical operations, rather frequently in fact. Watson urges us to remember that the world is a very large place, with trillions of living creatures in it, including the rose-chafers of mountainous Switzerland. Jung, offering us a brief history of his fascination with synchronous events, writes in *On Synchronicity* (S, 437) that certain of the coincidences he observed during the course of his life were so remarkable "that their 'chance' concurrence would represent a degree of improbability that would have to be expressed by an astronomical figure." Well, as a preliminary reply to *just this aspect* of Jung's theory, we would say simply that such things, involving just such "astronomical" odds, do in fact occur, and on a regular basis. "Events as rare as one in a million *do* happen," Watson (103) instructs us again:

> The truth is, in fact, that rare events are happening all the time. If that sounds paradoxical, remember it is a large world . . . Perhaps the most 'unlikely' gambling story that actually happened was when the 'even' [roulette] number came up at a Monte Carlo casino *28 times* in succession . . . This configuration, it has been calculated, would occur by chance once every 268, 435, 456 times–*but it happened*. Mathematician Warren Weaver worked out, from the number of casinos and number of players each day, that, on average, this event should take place every 500 years at Monte Carlo. Rare events do happen.

Of particular interest here, however, is that Watson's treatise, in one place, addresses itself specifically to a certain *kind* of coincidental occurrence from which Jung sought to derive substantial support for his views.

Jung informs us in his *Foreword to the 'I Ching'* (F, 192-193) that

> synchronicity takes the coincidence of events in space and time as meaning something more than mere chance, namely, a peculiar interdependence of objective events among themselves as well as with the subjective (psychic) states of the observer or observers.

He goes on:

> the ancient Chinese mind contemplates the cosmos in a way comparable to that of the modern physicist, who cannot deny that his model of the world is a decidedly psychophysical structure. The microphysical event includes the observer just as much as the reality underlying the *I Ching* comprises subjective, i.e., psychic conditions in the totality of the momentary situation. Just as causality describes the sequence of events, so synchronicity to the Chinese mind deals with the coincidence of events.

And then,

> The causal point of view tells us a dramatic story about how D came into existence: it took its origin from C, which existed before D, and C in turn had a father, B, etc. The synchronistic view on the other hand tries to produce an equally meaningful picture of coincidence. How does it happen that A', B', C' and D', etc. *appear all at the same moment and in the same place?* It happens in the first place because the physical events A' and B' are of the same quality as the psychic events C' and D', and further because all are the exponents of one and the same momentary situation. (my emphasis)

Jung insists upon adhering to the view that physical and psychic "qualities" share some sort of "sameness" despite his recognition that "causal connection can be determined statistically and can be subjected to experiment [while] experimenting with synchronicity seems to be impossible under ordinary conditions" (193). Jung is interested, then, in *patterns, sequences, series* of "acausality" and not simply in isolated, one-on-one coincidences. This is, of course, the very same topic that drew the attention of Paul Kammerer during the early twentieth century, and the attention of Arthur Koestler more recently (see Watson 1981, 14). Jung studied Kammerer but wrote his *Synchronicity* well before Koestler's work appeared–and not only appeared, by the way, but dismissed Jung's theory as muddled.

Now, Peter Watson (1981, 102) offers us in the treatise at which we've been looking a pattern, or sequence, of coincidence that answers Jung's formulations down to the final prime, and beyond, without requiring us to postulate any sort of "psychic quality" residing in events, or better, between events. In other words, Watson's instance, although amazing, is perfectly straightforward, perfectly comprehensible in naturalistic terms, perfectly capable of standing on its own empirical feet, if the reader will excuse so monstrous a metaphor. Writes Watson,

> Beatrice, Nebraska, is a small farming town, little more than a village and very religious. On 1 March 1950, choir practice was set for 7:20 in the evening. The minister, however, was a little late that night. His wife and daughter were members of the choir, and he waited while his wife finished ironing their daughter's dress. A fourth member of the choir, a girl, was also late: she wanted to finish a geometry problem . . . Two other choir members were late because their car would not start. And two others stayed home to hear the end of a particularly interesting radio program. In fact, all fifteen members of the Beatrice choir were late that night: not one arrived before 7:30. Which was just as well, because at 7:25 an explosion destroyed the entire church . . . Let us assume that any *one* chorister would be late about one choir practice in four . . . In other

words, there is a one in four chance that *one* member . . . would be late
on any given night. Now in this case there were actually ten reasons
which delayed the fifteen members . . . (for instance, the dress in need of
ironing was a single reason that delayed three members . . .). We can
say that the probability of everybody being late on the same night is
one-fourth . . . or 1/1,048, 576. This is the same as saying that there is
about one chance in a million that the ten reasons would all crop up on
the same night.

Not only is this particular pattern of coincidence Watson's "favourite," it
is also one that we can understand, in Watson's (102) words, "without any
suggestion of paranormal activity." A synchronistic *pattern* is no more
esoteric than a discrete synchronistic event.

Let me hasten to say here that I do not intend by all this to account for
every remarkable coincidence in the history of the planet down to the
present hour. Not only would that be impossible, not only would all kinds
of titillating examples immediately suggest themselves as they do in
Watson (1981, 132) and Koestler (1978, 270) both of whom concede the
ultimate mysteriousness of the universe, it would also be *superfluous*. I
mean, my aim as I announced it in the opening section of this book is not
to refute Jung's theory; it is, rather, to offer a psychoanalytic *alternative*.
Surely it is enough to observe that rare events do happen, everywhere, all
the time, and without necessitating supernatural explanation, if our purpose is to demonstrate along naturalistic lines the way in which such rare
events can trigger the *emotional response* that, for Jung, comprises the
synchronistic experience in its entirety. If we can perceive Jung's *beetle* in
naturalistic terms, we can perceive *enough* to continue; we can perceive
enough in the so-called objective realm to forge the empirical, psychoanalytic account of synchronicity that is our chief concern. We will have, on
the one hand, the confident recognition that remarkable coincidences do
happen in our world. We will not be "thrown" by them, or "spooked" by
them. We will not be prone to start looking for the paranormal because
something unlikely has occurred. Jungian synchronicity will not yank us in
through coincidence. On the other hand, we will have an entirely naturalistic explanation, rooted in personal, ontogenetic factors, of the *emotional
response* (including spiritual conviction) that may arise when a coincidence leads to a belief in synchronicity. We will not require anything
archetypal, anything phylogenetic, anything beyond the material in front of
our nose, to grasp the essential, underlying nature of the reaction. Both
sides of the problem will emerge straightforwardly, and meet.

DEFINITIONAL DIFFICULTIES

Let's turn more directly, now, to the theoretical, definitional side of synchronistic occurrences as they are depicted in the writings of Jung and his followers. Jung declares in *On Synchronicity: An Acausal Connecting Principle* (S, 444-45),

> synchronistic events rest on the *simultaneous occurrence of two different psychic states*. One of them is the normal, probable state (i.e. the one that is causally explicable), and the other, the critical experience, is the one that cannot be derived causally from the first ... An unexpected content which is directly or indirectly connected with some objective external event coincides with the ordinary psychic state: this is what I call synchronicity ... Synchronistic phenomena cannot in principle be associated with any conceptions of causality.

Jung has in mind here, of course, the beetle: "the scarab dream is a conscious representation arising from an unconscious, already existing image of the situation that will occur on the following day, i.e., the recounting of the dream and the appearance of the rose-chafer" (447). What has *not* happened yet, what is "remote in space and time" (447) is somehow "acausally" related to what is about to happen, in the consulting room. "Every emotional state produces an alteration of consciousness which Janet called *abaissement de niveau mental*," Jung proceeds to observe (447); and then,

> there is a certain narrowing of consciousness and a corresponding strengthening of the unconscious which, particularly in the case of strong affects, is noticeable even to the layman. The tone of the unconscious is heightened, thereby creating a gradient for the unconscious to flow toward the conscious. The conscious then comes under the influence of unconscious instinctual impulses and contents. These are as a rule complexes whose ultimate basis is the archetype, the 'instinctual pattern.' The unconscious also contains subliminal perceptions (as well as forgotten memory images that cannot be reproduced at the moment, or perhaps at all). Among the subliminal contents we must distinguish perceptions from what I would call an inexplicable 'knowledge,' or an 'immediacy' of psychic images. Whereas sense-perceptions can be related to probable or possible sensory stimuli below the threshold of consciousness, this 'knowledge,' or the 'immediacy' of unconscious images, either has no recognizable foundation, or else we find there are causal connections with certain already existing, and often archetypal, contents. But these images, whether rooted in an already existing basis or not, stand in a analogous or equivalent (i.e., meaningful) relationship

to objective occurrences which have no recognizable or even conceiv-
able causal relationship with them.

"How," Jung (447) demands, with the beetle in the forefront of his mind,
"could an event remote in space and time produce a corresponding psychic
image when the transmission of energy necessary for this is not even
thinkable?" Jung then concludes as follows: "however incomprehensible it
may appear, we are finally compelled to assume that there is in the unconscious something like an *a priori* knowledge or an 'immediacy' of events
which lacks any causal basis" (447). Allow me to pose a few questions for
the reader at this juncture.

On what *basis*, exactly, does Jung ask us (twice) to relinquish *unconscious memory* as a *causal* explanation of synchronistic occurrences? On
what basis, exactly, does Jung ask us (twice) to rule out *sensorial perceptions* as the source of all unconscious imagery? On what basis, exactly,
does Jung ask us to accept that "emotional states" (like those felt in
synchronicity) precipitate the dispatch of "archetypal contents" and "*a
priori* knowledge" and "immediate [or phylogenetic] images" to the
conscious mind, as opposed to mnemic traces or simple associations
arising from our actual, personal experience in the world? What is it, in
short, that "compels" us to *exclude* synchronicity from the rest of our
human behavior which is "causally" rooted in perception and memory?
Has Jung *explored* the early period in which our *emotional lives* have their
origin? Has he gone among infants and children to *see* the manner in
which perception and memory develop to leave indelible traces on our
affective natures? Has he *endeavored* through the direct observation of
young people to distinguish what is ontogenetic or experiential from what
is "archetypal" or "immediate"? Has he attempted to find these things out
before *asserting* that synchronicity has no recognizable *cause* in the
customary sense of the word, as well as in the specialized psychoanalytic
sense that involves the unconscious? Jung *claims* that he must drop
ordinary causality because the "scarab dream" and the oracular episode in
his office are "remote in space and time." They force him to rely on the
acausal realm, on archetypes, on *a priori* knowledge, on immediate
images, and the rest. But this *claim* is precisely what Jung is obliged to
prove. He *assumes* the inexplicable remoteness of the events; he *assumes*
there is no other way to explain them, and he then *uses* that to dismiss
perception and memory, and move to the archetypal. Jung has it *backwards*. He must *demonstrate the truth* of the synchronistic moment *before*
he can claim its special, determining stature. Needless to say, Jung is
aware of the problem, its hugeness, its decisiveness. As I've already

suggested, he touches on it *twice*: is synchronicity based upon *real memories*? Is synchronicity an aspect of *sensorial perceptions*, like everything else in the bodily world? If he lets perceptual reality in, he must let it in *all the way* and watch it gobble up the archetypal stuff: what *is* archetypal and what *isn't* archetypal as far as synchronicity is concerned? Jung can't go *that* route, for it would make it impossible to sort anything out with genuine assurance. Indeed, it would turn Jung into a kind of phenomenologist, involved in the hopeless task of categorizing a vast array of mental contents. The reader knows perfectly well, of course, the answers to the questions posed a moment earlier: Jung ignored the early period; he idealized children; he *never looked* at the origins of perception and memory, let alone their developmental significance; he turned *away*, to the collective unconscious, and archetypes, and *a priori* knowledge, and immediate imagery–the Platonic world of eternal forms, the mythological world of heroes and gods. Jung was unable to see the purchase of perception and memory on synchronicity because he knew nothing about perception and memory as they are rooted in the life of infancy and childhood. It was all "incomprehensible" because Jung had nothing in his investigations as a psychologist to make it otherwise, as we will strive eventually to do.

We cannot say with absolute assurance, of course, why Jung turned away from infancy and childhood, why he failed to ground his theory of synchronicity in the tangible, empirical realm as we usually conceive of it. Charet (1993, 298) maintains that "Jung, during his early life, came under the influence of certain experiences and beliefs that are characteristic of Spiritualism. Spiritualism later provided him with a religious framework within which he could fit his extraordinary experiences. While he ventured into philosophy and then psychiatry in order to more adequately account for such experiences, these approaches did not completely satisfy him. When Jung moved to create a general psychology he sought to incorporate such religious experiences into psychological molds which he termed archetypes." Although "he identified himself as an empirical scientist," concludes Charet (297), "[Jung] seems in his later formulations on the nature of the archetype to have moved beyond the borders of science." Be that as it may, Jung elects to approach synchronistic events by looking into what he calls "the obscurest corners," by "summoning up the courage" to "shock the prejudices" of his scientific age (S, 448). Instead of relying upon the actual, developmental lives of actual, living, breathing human beings–the most obvious, natural place for a *psychiatrist* to go–he concentrates his attention upon the astrological charts of Herbert von Kloeckler, the medieval tracts (on magic) of Albertus Magnus, alchemical hypotheses, Chinese and other books of divination, the highly speculative, paradoxical world of quantum physics and Einsteinean relativity, the ESP and PK experiments of J.B. Rhine, and even upon reports of near-death experiences, mystical levitations, and something called "transcerebral thought" (S, 511). The result, I believe I can say with impunity, comes very close to confusion, both for Jung and for the reader. Just listen (S, 511):

> synchronicity is not a phenomenon whose regularity is at all easy to demonstrate ... [The] synchronistic factor merely stipulates the existence of an intellectually necessary principle which could be added as a fourth to the recognized triad of space, time, and causality ... Synchronistic phenomena are found to occur–experimentally–with some degree of regularity and frequency in the intuitive, 'magical' procedures, where they are subjectively convincing but are extremely difficult to verify objectively and cannot be statistically evaluated (at least at present).

And then, a few sentences later (S, 512-13),

> synchronicity is not a philosophical view but an empirical concept which postulates an intellectually necessary principle. This cannot be called either materialism or metaphysics ... Just as the introduction of time as the fourth dimension in modern physics postulates an irrepresentable space-time continuum, so the idea of synchronicity with its inherent quality of meaning produces a picture of the world so irrepresentable as to be completely baffling. The advantage, however, of adding this concept is that it makes possible a view which includes the psychoid factor in our description and knowledge of nature–that is an *a priori* meaning or 'equivalence.' The problem that runs like a red thread through the speculations of alchemists for fifteen hundred years thus repeats and solves itself, the so-called axiom of Maria the Jewess (or Copt): 'Out of the Third comes the One as the Fourth.'

What is "baffling" here, I submit, is the whole presentation. Who knows what it means? Colin Wilson (1984, 114) suggests that Jung is attempting to "blind us with science." One might add, science and lots of other things too. Arthur Koestler (1972, 97-8, 101) writes of Jung's "obscure meanderings" as follows: "one cannot help being reminded of the biblical mountain whose labors gave birth to a mouse." Let's listen to another passage or two, just to be sure we have a good "feel" for the material (S, 515):

> It [synchronicity] consists essentially of 'chance' equivalencies. Their *tertium comparationis* [i.e. subtle body] rests on the psychoid factors I

call archetypes. These are *indefinite*, that is to say, they can be known and determined only approximately. Although associated with causal processes, or 'carried' by them, they continually go beyond their frame of reference, an infringement to which I would give the name 'transgressivity,' because the archetypes are not found exclusively in the psychic sphere but can occur just as much in circumstances that are not psychic.

And again (S, 516),

synchronicity in the narrow sense is only a particular instance of general acausal orderliness–that, namely, of the equivalence of psychic and physical processes where the observer is in the fortunate position of being able to recognize the *tertium comparationis*. But as soon as he perceives the archetypal background he is tempted to trace the mutual assimilation of independent psychic and physical processes back to a (causal) effect of the archetype, and thus to overlook the fact that they are merely contingent. This danger is avoided if one regards synchronicity as a special instance of general acausal orderliness. In this way, we avoid multiplying our principles of explanation illegitimately, for the archetype *is* the introspectively recognizable form of *a priori* psychic orderliness. If an external process now associates itself with it, it falls into the same basic pattern–in other words, it too is 'ordered.'

Surely, after reading material like this, even the most dedicated, sympathetic reader might feel inclined to throw up his hands. Does Jung (S, 531) himself feel so inclined when he writes toward the end of his lengthy treatise that

the term [synchronicity] explains nothing [;] it simply formulates the occurrence of meaningful coincidences which, in themselves, are chance happenings but are so improbable that we must assume them to be based on some kind of principle, or some property of the empirical world[?]

Perhaps. We certainly have come a long, long way to be left with "some kind of principle" or "some property."

But what of Jung's disciples, what of those who have taken up synchronicity during the past half century? Surely they are able to rectify the master's shortcomings, to guide us to a clear, straightforward understanding of synchronous events. Alas, it is not the case. Because they are prone to follow Jung's leads, indeed to reflect his appetite for phylogenetic assumptions and speculative excursions into the realm of modern physics, they simply do not take us further than Jung himself takes us. While their *writing* is less tortured than Jung's, their *ideas* are just as fuzzy, just as confusional. It is all amplification, amplification and gloss. Let's have a brief look.

For F. David Peat (1987, 111), the key resides in "the symbols and images of the collective unconscious," a "realm that lies beyond space, time, and matter." Psychically, we "descend" into a "dark passageway" and "emerge" near "an underground ocean" in which "all minds have their origin." Here we find "the wellspring of synchronicity."

For Combs and Holland (1990, 32), the holographic theories of physicist David Bohm harbor the key:

> the deep well of the superimplicate breathes forth meaning which might rightly be termed mythic into the wide world of physical and mental reality. From this perspective there is no fundamental enigma in synchronicity.

Apparently Combs and Holland do not detect a contradiction when they write toward the end of their joint effort that synchronicity "cannot be grasped with the rational mind." It must be "lived with one's whole being." We must "surrender to it;" we must "let it wash over and benignly carry us" (144). Did Combs write the scientific chapters of this book and Holland the romantic ones? Or is it the other way around?

According to Jungian analyst Edward Edinger (1972,101), at whose influential work we've already glanced, "Jung is calling 'God' what most people call chance or accident." For enlightened Jungians, in fact, chance does not even "exist." Everything has "meaning;" everything is expressive of "transpersonal patterns and powers." Were we to become more "primitive," more "child-like" in the sense Jung intends for those terms, we would appreciate this. Edinger (101) concludes by writing, "perhaps this is the meaning of Jesus' saying, 'unless you turn and become like children you will never enter the Kingdom of Heaven.'"

For another famous Jungian analyst and theoretician, C.A. Meier (1986, 183-84), "the field of synchronicity" is "analogous to Einstein's work in the field of relativity." One day, suggests Meier, "it will become necessary" to develop a "general theory" which will account for the behavior of the physical world on the one hand and for the behavior of the "psycho-physical" world on the other hand. By "psycho-physical" world Meier has in mind the "mantic," the prophetic, the realm of oracular divination, as found in the *I Ching* for example.

The scholarly Robert Aziz (1990, 58-9) also finds the key in Einstein's work, through "archetypal" considerations, of course. "In the microphysical world of the archetype," he writes, "space and time are inseparably linked in a four-dimensional space-time continuum." The term "synchronicity" must be used "specifically to describe the acausal connecting principle in the space-time world of the archetype." The "synchronistic event, in contrast to this, takes place in the space- and time-bound world of ego-consciousness." I'll leave it to the reader to figure that distinction out.

Victor Mansfield (1995, 82) joins the parade of Einsteinean-quantum babble with the "wave function" held high. "The role of the archetype in synchronicity," he informs us, "parallels the role of the wave function in quantum mechanics," for an "archetype is a probability structure in the psyche." The archetype represents "psychic probability" or "a range of possible synchronicity experiences." Never mind that "neither the wave function nor the archetypes are directly observable."

In Ira Progoff's (1973, 74) view,

> the master principle of the cosmos is . . . not something that can be analyzed or measured. It is a subtle, hidden principle of correspondence that is somehow inherent in the patterning of the world. It is a principle that has had a fuller development in the East than in the West, but by the time Leibniz used it (ca 1700), it already had a substantial European history. Jung has drawn upon this history for the contents of his concept, and stressing the pattern of each particular moment of time, has given it the name Synchronicity.

Are we inching back toward Jung's indefiniteness, toward his allusion at the close of his treatise (S, 531) to "some kind of principle" or "some property" that is involved in synchronistic occurrences?

Writes Jean Bolen (1982, 84), present-day Jungian therapist and New Age guru:

> with the idea of synchronicity, psychology joined hands with parapsychology and theoretical physics in seeing an underlying 'something' akin to what the mystic has been seeing all along. The important element that synchronicity adds is a dimension of personal meaning that acknowledges what a person intuitively feels when a synchronistic event is directly experienced. Theories and laboratory experiences make thinkable the idea of an underlying invisible connection between everything in the universe. But when it is an intuitively felt experience, a spiritual element enters.

We have come full circle, then; we are back to a mystical "something," back to a "spiritual element," back to a kind of "invisible connection" that ties everything to everything else. We even find the notion of parapsychology in Bolen–clairvoyance, telepathy, psychokinesis, and the rest–just as we discovered that notion in Jung's treatise, *On Synchronicity: An Acausal Connecting Principle* (S, 511). I will be treating all of these works more fully in later sections, but the gist of the matter resides in the citations I've chosen.

It is time to explain synchronicity from a realistic psychological standpoint, to rely upon *only* the actual experience of actual people in the real world, to set aside all the assumptive phylogenetic materials, to divorce synchronicity from its dubious marriage to quantum physics and Einsteinean relativity, to shed the esoterica and arcanum–in short, to *look* and to *see* how synchronicity is rooted in the individual's actual developmental past and how it manifests itself as a naturalistic psychological reflection of that past. There is no mysterious "something" here, no "subtle body," no hidden "process" or "principle" waiting for our discovery. There is only the human being expressing his/her fantasies, wishes, and fears. There is only the human being presenting the human reality as it is lived through over and over again each day by the inhabitants of the planet. It is time to offer an *alternative* to the Jungian account of synchronicity.

NOTE

1. Here is the key to Chapter One's references to the works of Jung (except for letters which are indicated by date):

ACU	Archetypes of the Collective Unconscious
F	Foreword to the *I Ching*
FP	Freud and Psychoanalysis
S	Synchronicity: An Acausal Connecting Principle
ST	Symbols of Transformation

REFERENCES

Aziz, R. 1990. C.G. Jung's Psychology of Religion and Synchronicity. Albany: State University of New York Press.

Bolen, J. 1982. *The Tao of Psychology: Synchronicity and the Self.* San Francisco: Harper and Row.

Charet, F. 1993. *Spiritualism and the Foundation of C.G. Jung's Psychology.* Albany: State University of New York Press.

Combs, A. and Holland, M. 1990. *Synchronicity: Science, Myth, and the Trickster.* New York: Paragon House.

Edinger, E. 1972. *Ego and Archetype: Individuation and the Religious Function of the Psyche.* New York: G.P. Putnam's Sons.

Feibleman, J. 1976. *Understanding Oriental Philosophy.* New York: Horizon Press.

Horgan, J. 1996. "Why Freud Isn't Dead." *Scientific American,* December, pp. 106-11.

Houston, J. 1996. *A Mythic Life: Learning to Live Our Greater Story.* New York: HarperCollins.

Hughes, E. 1971. *Chinese Philosophy in Classical Times.* London: J.M. Dent.

Jung, C. 1970. *Symbols of Transformation. Collected Works,* vol. 5. Princeton: Princeton University Press.

———. 1973. *Letters,* vols. 1 and 2. Princeton: Princeton University Press.

———. 1976. "The Father in the Destiny of the Individual." In *Freud and Psychoanalysis. Collected Works,* vol. 4. Princeton: Princeton University Press.

———. 1981. *On Synchronicity: An Acausal Connecting Principle.* In *The Structure and Dynamics of the Psyche. Collected Works,* vol. 8. Princeton: Princeton University Press.

———. 1986. "Foreword to the *'I Ching'.*" In *Psychology and the East.* London: Routledge and Kegan Paul.

———. 1990. *Archetypes of the Collective Unconscious. Collected Works,* vol. 9, part 1. Princeton: Princeton University Press.

Kaminer, W. 1996. "The Latest Fashion in Irrationality." *Atlantic Monthly,* July, pp. 103-6.

Koestler, A. 1972. *The Roots of Coincidence.* New York: Random House.

———. 1978. *Janus: A Summing Up.* New York: Random House.

Mansfield, V. 1995. *Synchronicity, Science, and Soul-Making.* Chicago: Open Court.

Meier, C. 1986. *Soul and Body: Essays on the Theories of C.G. Jung.* San Francisco: Lapis Press.

Peat, F. 1987. *Synchronicity: The Bridge Between Matter and Mind.* New York: Bantam Books.

Peck, S. 1988. *The Road Less Traveled.* New York: Simon and Schuster.

Progoff, I. 1973. *Jung, Synchronicity, and Human Destiny: C.G. Jung's Theory of Meaningful Coincidence.* New York: Julian Press.

Redfield, J. 1993. *The Celestine Prophecy: An Adventure.* New York: Warner Books.

Singer, J. 1972. *Boundaries of the Soul: The Practice of Jung's Psychology.* New York: Viking Press.

Storr, A. 1973. *C.G. Jung.* New York: Viking Press.

Watson, P. 1981. *Twins: An Uncanny Relationship?* New York: Viking Press.

Wilhelm, H. 1973. *Eight Lectures on the 'I Ching.'* Princeton: Princeton University Press.

Wilson, C. 1984. *C.G. Jung: Lord of the Underworld.* Wellingborough: Aquarian Press.

2

The Psychoanalytic Matrix
of Synchronistic Events

A NEW PROVINCE OF KNOWLEDGE

In the next few pages, I will describe a revolution in human understanding. This revolution has been going on for about one hundred years; it harbors an enormous potential for improving human relations, indeed, human existence generally; it has catalyzed and continues to catalyze major changes in our private and public conduct both as children and adults; and finally, it allows us to discern the motivational dynamics not only of synchronicity as we know it today but of a great many other spiritual beliefs and ideas throughout the world. I am referring to the comprehensive study of human infancy and childhood.

Until recently, babies were routinely operated upon without anesthetics because the doctors believed the babies did not feel pain. Astounding as that may seem it is not untypical of the ignorance and insensitivity that Westerners have displayed toward infants over the centuries. If the reader has an appetite for this horror story, I refer him to the work of those psycho-historians who have been devoting themselves to the subject for about thirty years (see de Mause 1982). Although the mistreatment of babies is still a common occurrence, and may always be common given the tendency of people to transfer their frustrations and discontentments to their offspring, we are at last beginning to grasp in some depth what might be called the nature of the infant's special world.

It will be my contention in this chapter, as it is my contention in this book, that we cannot grasp the nature of the spiritual apart from this new and revolutionary knowledge. Unless we are willing to view the spiritual realm as addressing, or attempting to resolve, the dilemmas of infancy and childhood, we will simply miss out. Our understanding will not merely be partial; it will be hopelessly flawed, hopelessly incomplete. That is the nature of genuine revolutions: they change perceptions, and they leave behind those who are unable or unwilling to have their perceptions changed.

Psychoanalysis was instrumentally bound up, of course, with the advent of this revolution, and because psychoanalysis was a new discipline with huge and difficult territories to chart, and many original minds were involved in the charting, the revolution went forward amidst considerable controversy. Although Freud made important contributions to the understanding of infantile sexuality and narcissism, his own personal resistance to the study of the mother-infant bond, as well as his preoccupation with the Oedipus complex (the second resulted in some measure from the first), discouraged investigators from examining meticulously the psychological realities of the early period. However, by the 1930's through the pioneering work of Melanie Klein and her followers, and by the 1950's through the work of Winnicott, Fairbairn, and Bowlby, significant and permanent inroads were being made into this new province of knowledge. People were beginning to appreciate in earnest the degree to which the mind and the emotions are shaped, even determined, by the original relationship between the parent and the child.

I am not suggesting that controversy ceased after Freud's resistances were skirted. There was still disagreement, and there will always be disagreement given the problematical nature of the subject and the difficulty of devising so-called objective measures. Does the relation between mother and infant govern the nature and growth of the instinctual endowment? Can what psychoanalysis calls "instinct theory" be reconciled with what it calls "object relations theory"? *Are* there instincts at all in any true sense of the word? What is the father's role during the formative years? And what about changing patterns of infant care? Such questions are raised routinely in a variety of psychoanalytic publications; obviously, we are not going to resolve them here once and for all. What we can underscore, however, is that by the present day a remarkable consensus has emerged on the importance of merger and separation as a key psychological conflict of the early period.

INTERNALIZED RELATIONSHIPS

During the first two decades of this century psychoanalysis concentrated it efforts primarily upon repression, and upon the relation of repression to the dynamic unconscious. As Freud viewed the matter, the requirements of civilized existence obliged the individual's sexual and aggressive tendencies, or more correctly, the individual's sexual and aggressive "drives," to "go under," to manifest themselves but partially, in an "inhibited" way. The tension between one's urgent instinctual demands and their truncated expression in culture led in a good many instances to "neurotic" disorders with repression at their center and in *all* instances, for *all* people, to a life of "discontent" and conflict. It was through slips of the tongue, free associations, organic and behavioral symptoms, and above all through dreams that such conflicts and discontentments revealed themselves to the "analyst of the psyche." As he continued to work with people, however, Freud came increasingly to recognize the extent to which the problem of neurosis involved not merely the repression of instinct, the struggle between nature and culture, unconscious and conscious experience, but the extent to which one's *conscious* life, lived primarily at the level of ego processes, was itself a vehicle for the expression of unconscious aims. By the mid to late 1920's, in fact, Freud had come to regard "anxiety" as the "main problem of neurosis" (Freud 1959, 69-71) and "separation from the protecting mother" as the chief cause of "anxiety" (Freud 1974, 47-8). He had shifted away from a "drive model" to a relational model, one in which the relational field or the relational configuration is of paramount importance. Such a relational model does not deny, of course, the significance of human instincts or human biological tendencies, including temperament. It merely suggests that instinct is not implacably formational. What the individual brings innately to the world both shapes and is *shaped by* the environment.

From the inception of his career, Freud (1971, 104) was scornful of psychology's readiness to deal *only* with the phenomena of consciousness. He regarded the "psychoanalytic assumption of unconscious mental activity" as an "extension of the corrections begun by Kant in regard to our views on external perception." Just as Kant "warned us not to overlook the fact that our perception is subjectively conditioned and must not be regarded as identical with the phenomena perceived," so psychoanalysis "bids us not to set conscious perception in the place of the unconscious mental process which is its object." The "mental," like the "physical," is "not necessarily in reality just what it appears to us to be." Still, Freud (104) concluded, it is gratifying to discover that the "correction of inner perception" does not "present difficulties so great as that of outer perception," that the "inner object" is "less hard to discern truly than is the outside world." Freud gives us here, for the first time in Western intellectual history, not merely two kinds of philosophical objects, those of the inner and those of the outer world, but an *inner object with an unconscious, dynamic, perceptual dimension.*

Psychoanalysis, as an originator of knowledge and understanding, culminates in our full appreciation of the significance of *internalization* in human life. It has long been stressed, perhaps to the point of becoming a cliché, that man is distinguished from the other animals by his proclivity to create and to dwell within a world of symbols, that his existence must not be regarded dualistically as of the mind over here and of the body over there but must be grasped in terms of his psychobiological propensity to unite mind and feeling in a symbolic mode of expression. Indeed, the entire shape of modern philosophy, anthropology, and sociology is importantly determined by its concentration upon the symbolic style of social and individual organization. Yet to stress this aspect of our behavior is to stress what is merely a visible, "higher" manifestation of a considerably more basic human tendency. As we concentrate upon the nature of internalization we find ourselves in possession of a more powerful analytic instrument than that which inheres in the symbolistic approach–which deals, if the truth were told, with materials that take shape *after* the elemental events of our lives have transpired. I do not believe we can genuinely grasp the symbolic–including the symbols of the spiritual realm– without first having grasped the psychoanalytic, and by psychoanalytic I do not mean the libido theory, the Oedipus complex, the classical "Freudian" scheme. I mean, rather, those close, post-Freudian investigations of the infant-mother symbiosis which have occurred within the past four decades and which are offered to the reader in detail during the course of this chapter as we ready ourselves in earnest for a psychoanalysis of Jungian synchronicity.

The human infant, perhaps from the inception of his extrauterine life, evinces a powerful urge to internalize the universe around him, to take in and to retain a sizable portion of the materials with which he comes into contact during the long course of his development toward childhood. It is customary in psychoanalytic circles to approach the problem of internalization by referring to introjection, incorporation, and identification. We do not have to worry too much about these terms here, but it is probably a good idea to mention that introjection and incorporation are generally regarded as the kinds of "primitive" or pre-cognitive internalizing processes that are employed by the infant and the pre-Oedipal child, the adolescent, and the adult. I say "generally regarded" because the child, the adolescent, and the adult retain (and often express) the capacity to incorporate and introject other persons and things in a deep, tenacious, "primitive" way when circumstances provoke intense psychological pressure and recall the aims and wishes of life's early stages. Indeed, as I will soon work to establish, Jungian thought as a whole may be considered a striking exemplification of *just this point.* "All those processes" by which we "transform real or imagined interactions" with the environment, and "real or imagined characteristics of the environment" into *inner* relationships and *inner* characteristics might be thought of as that to which the term *internalization* refers (Schafer 1968, 8-9)

We must note in this connection that the tendency to internalize the environment is prompted by *both* the developing cortex and the growing organism's *defensive needs.* It is the infant's helpless condition, his long period of dependency, his anxiety over separation and loss, along with his accompanying urge to master, to control, a world that is frequently at odds with his wishes and threatening in itself, that goads the internalizing process to life. What we have here is in large measure a kind of "magical" activity based on the feeling-belief that one is safe only when vital external objects and relationships (including paradoxically "bad" objects and relationships) are *taken and held inside.* Of particular importance in all of this, of course, is the caretaker.

That the child's interaction with the parent is the foundation of human psychology everyone appreciates in a "soft," general way. What I wish to emphasize here is that the child's interaction with the parent is the foundation of human psychology in a "hard," structural, perceptual sense that has yet to be recognized by large numbers of people. Internalization transpires at the sensorial, *bodily* level. The materials that are taken in–and these are largely aspects of the caretaker– are taken into the child's *perceiving organism.* It is there that they root themselves, and it is there that they remain, for the duration of the individual's life. In the remarks of Freud, cited earlier, Kant was called explicitly to mind. We must call him to mind again here by declaring that the very *a priori* ground of our perceptual participation in the world is connected inextricably to the internalization of the early period in which the parental object functions as the dynamic, emotive center of the neonate's existence. It is in this perceptual-structural context that I may begin to suggest what the psychoanalytic term "object" refers to.

It is used to indicate the child "care-giver," the individual who accompanies the child through all the successive stages of development. This person is, first of all, a partner in a variety of reflexive, biological urges and responses; she/he then becomes a "somebody" who can be recognized and represented, as well as respected, feared, hated, needed, and loved. With regard to the perceptual complexity embedded in this general picture, "object" may refer to the *breast* that provides appetitive pleasure or frustration, to the *person* who provides the breast, to the *perception* of the person, and to the psychical *representation* of that perception. In subsequent sections I range among these distinctions, relying upon the reader to apprehend the nuance of the moment. The extent to which such "objects," through the process of internalization, come to be integrally bound up with the individual's existence is captured dramatically by the current trend in psychoanalysis to refer to a person's "selfobjects" when probing into issues of identity formation and conflict-inducing situations. It is precisely here that we find the deepest meaning of the psychoanalytic commonplace that virtually all relationships between human beings contain an element of the transference, that is, an unconscious element tied developmentally to significant figures of the past. Behind the transference stand the primary internalizations of the early period. Those "inner objects" of Freud's essay, then, are not entirely "inner" or "mental" in the customary sense, the sense he had in mind. They have a kind of physical or "objective" existence in the body. As for the "objects" of the "outside world" also mentioned by Freud, they themselves are not entirely external or "physical"–again in the sense he had in mind; for they are "colored" or projectively "touched" by the perceiving organism with which they come into contact.

SEPARATION AND MERGER

The conflict between separation and merger not only dominates the life of the infant but extends itself far beyond infancy and childhood into the life of the adolescent and adult. It revolves around the struggle to become an autonomous, separate person, differentiated and distinct, and, *at the same time*, to retain one's connection to significant others–either the actual parents or their later substitutes in a protean variety of shapes and forms. For the human creature, two of life's most powerful needs are, paradoxically, to be attached and to be separate, to be related and to be independent, to be autonomous and to be connected, and it is precisely this paradoxical and in some sense contradictory thrust in human growth and development, this antithetical, two-sided inclination of people, that makes human behavior so problematical, so maddeningly difficult to see and to fathom, and that brings so much confusion to the lives of individuals and societies. Ethel Person (1989, 132), in her wonderful book *Dreams of Love*

and Fateful Encounters, renders the matter this way: "The self is deline-
ated only through separation, but the sense of being separated proves
impossible to bear. The solitary self feels cut off, alone, without resources.
The solitary self feels impelled to merge with a new object." What Dr.
Person has captured, if I may be permitted to indicate the issue still again,
is that the *two* needs, to be separate and joined, independent and connected, are from a deep psychological angle *one* need neither side of which
finds expression without engaging the other, like a crab going backwards
and forwards at the same time. When the desire for merger is felt it
typically engages the need to be separate; and the need to be separate
engages the wish to be connected, joined. While it is easy to write about
the matter, to employ such terms as alogical, paradoxical, and antithetical,
it can be most unpleasant to experience the actual conflict when it occurs,
along with the inner confusion that it often engenders. I would suggest, in
fact, that we have here a major source of human stress.

From the many psychoanalytic accounts of infancy and childhood, of
the growth and development of the human creature, I choose what is
generally regarded as the most methodologically sophisticated, accurate,
and helpful, namely Margaret Mahler's *Psychological Birth of the Human
Infant* (1975). A child psychiatrist and pediatrician working with normal
children in a specially constructed facility in New York City during the
1950's and 60's, Mahler (and her associates) places the accent immediately on the struggle between separation and union.

We take for granted, she reminds us (Mahler 1975, 3), our experience
of ourselves as both fully "in" and fully separate from the "world out
there." Our consciousness of ourselves as distinct, differentiated entities
and our concomitant absorption into the external environment, without an
awareness of self, are the polarities between which we move with varying
ease, and with varying degrees of alternation or simultaneity. Yet the
establishment of such consciousness, such ordinary, taken-for-granted
awareness, is a slowly unfolding process that is not coincident in time with
our biological emergence from the womb. It is tied closely and developmentally to our dawning experience of the primary love object as also
separate in space, as having an existence of her/his own.[1] Moreover, the
struggle to achieve this "individuation" reverberates throughout the course
of our lives: "It is never finished; it remains always active; new phases of
the life cycle find new derivatives of the earliest processes still at work"
(3). As we shall see, Jung's theory of synchronicity is designed in large
measure to address certain specific derivatives of these "early processes."

What must be stressed in particular here is the strength of *both sides*
of the polarity. Children, with every move toward maturation, are con-

fronted with the threat of "object loss," with traumatic situations involving separation from the caregiver. Thus they are constantly tempted to draw back, to regress, to move *toward* the object and the old relation as opposed to *away* from the object and the anticipated future, the new reality. At the same time, the normally endowed child strives mightily to emerge from his early fusion (we could say confusion) with the mother, to *escape* and to *grow*. His individuation consists precisely of those developmental achievements, those increasing motor and mental accomplishments, that begin to mark his separate existence, his separate identity as a separate being. The ambivalent impulses toward and away from the object, the great urge to differentiate and at the same time stay connected, are in Mahler's words, forever intertwined (1975, 4), although they may proceed divergently, one or the other lagging behind or leaping ahead during a given period.

Mahler (1975, 4) makes plain that this process is not merely one of many equally important processes which transpire during the early time. On the contrary, the achievement of separation constitutes the very core of the self, the foundation of one's identity and being as a person. Yet this foundation can be gained (and here is the echo of a paradox again) only if the parent gives to the child a persistent, uninterrupted feeling of connection, of union–a tie that encourages the very breaking of it. This delicate balancing act is never perfect, and Mahler emphasizes throughout the course of her study that old conflicts over separation, old, unresolved issues of identity and bodily boundaries, can be reawakened or even remain active throughout the course of one's existence, at any or all stages of the life cycle. What appears to be a struggle for connection or distinctness in the now of one's experience can be the flare up of the ancient struggle in which one's self began to emerge from the orbit of the *magna mater*. We will shortly be exploring the degree to which this last observation sheds light upon synchronistic events.

By separation, then, Mahler does not mean primarily the physical separation of the baby in space or the distance from the caregiver, the kind of separation we associate, for example, with the work of John Bowlby. What Mahler has in mind is an *inward* or *intrapsychic separation* from both the mother and her extension, the world. The gradual development of this subjective awareness, this inward perception of the self and the other, leads eventually to clear, distinct inner representations of a "self" that is distinguished from "external objects." It is precisely this sense of being a separate individual that psychotic children are unable to achieve.

Similarly, when Mahler uses the term "symbiosis" the accent is not upon a behavioral state but an inward condition, a feature of primitive emotional life wherein the differentiation between the self and the mother has not occurred, or where a regression to an undifferentiated state has occurred. This does not necessarily require the presence of the mother; it can be based *on primitive images of oneness,* or *on a denial of perceptions that postulate separation.* Thus for Mahler (1975, 8), identity during the early period does not refer to the child having a sense of *who* he is; it refers to the child having a sense *that* he is. Indeed, the sense that he is can be regarded as the first step in the process of an unfolding individuality. The achievement of separation-individuation is a kind of "second birth," a "hatching" (9) from the symbiotic mother-infant "membrane" in which the child is originally contained.

THE STAGES OF DEVELOPMENT

Mahler (1975, 41) calls the earliest stage of development "autistic."[2] The infant "spends most of is day in a half-sleeping, half-waking state." He awakens mainly to feed and falls to sleep again when he is satisfied, or relieved of tensions. "Physiological rather than psychological processes are dominant," and the period as a whole is "best seen" in physiological terms. There is nothing abnormal about this "autism," as Mahler employs the term. The baby simply lacks awareness of the mother as a ministering agent and of himself as the object of her ministrations.

From the second month on, however, the baby increasingly feels the presence of the mother, and it is just this sense of the caretaker (or the "need-satisfying object") *being there* that marks the inception of the normal symbiotic phase, which reaches a peak of intensity at about six to nine months. The most remarkable feature of this phase (and one that will be of great significance for us as we study Jung's theory) is contained in Mahler's point that the infant "behaves and functions as though he and his mother were an omnipotent system–a dual unity with one common boundary" (1975, 44). The symbiotic infant participates emotionally and perceptually in a kind of delusional or hallucinatory fusion with the omnipotent mothering figure. Later in infancy and childhood, and indeed later in life at all stages when we experience severe stress, "this is the mechanism to which the ego regresses." Mahler hypothesizes that the symbiotic stage is "perhaps what Freud and Romain Rolland discussed in their dialogue as the sense of boundlessness of the oceanic feeling" (44). Psychoanalytic discussions of religion, and in particular of mystical states, generally begin with a reference to the Freud-Rolland exchange.

Thus, when the autistic phase subsides, or, to use the metaphors characteristic of Mahler's treatise, when the "autistic shell" has "cracked"

and the child can no longer "keep out external stimuli," a "second protec-
tive, yet selective and receptive shield" begins to develop in the form of
the symbiotic orbit, the mother and the child's dual-unity. While the
normal autistic phase serves postnatal physiological growth and homeosta-
sis, the normal symbiotic phase marks the all-important human capacity to
bring the mother into a psychic fusion that comprises "the primal soil from
which *all subsequent relationships form*" (1975, 48, my emphasis). We
commence our existence as people in the illusion that the other (who
appears to be omnipotent) is part of the self. Although the mother is
actually *out there*, ministering to the child, she is perceived by the latter to
be a facet of his own organism, his own primitive ego. What the mother
"magically" accomplishes in the way of care–the production of milk, the
provision of warmth, the sensation of security–the baby omnipotently
attributes to the mother and *to himself*. At the emotional, pre-verbal level
he declares, in effect, "I am not separate from my symbiotic partner; my
partner and I are one. Whatever my partner appears to possess and to do, I
possess and do as well. Whatever power my partner has, I also have. We
are *one,* one omnipotent indestructible unit, twin stars revolving around
each other in a single orbit of emotion and will." As D.W. Winnicott
(1974, 13) unforgettably expresses it, the feeling of omnipotence is so
strong in the infant (and so persistently clung to in the growing child when
the dual-unity of the symbiotic stage begins to break down) that it is
"nearly a fact."

What this means, of course, is that the decline of symbiosis, or the
increasing awareness of separation on the part of the child, will be experienced as a loss of *self*. If union with mother means wholeness, then dis-
union will mean less than wholeness. As Mahler phrases it elsewhere
(1968, 9), the cessation of the symbiotic phase marks the "loss of a part of
[one's] ego." Let us examine Mahler's account of this original human
trauma (the expulsion from paradise), and let us bear in mind as we
proceed, first, that the transition from symbiosis to individuation is a multi-
faceted, complex process that consumes the first three years of life, and
second, that for many, many people the loss of omnipotent merger and the
narcissistic gratification that goes with it is never entirely accepted at the
deep, unconscious level. I am not suggesting that the infant's growing
abilities and independence fail to provide him with satisfaction; to be sure,
they do, and Mahler is careful to emphasize *both* sides of the equation, the
drive to remain with and to relinquish the mother. I am suggesting only
that the movement away is attended by powerful anxiety and by the
irrational wish to have it *both* ways: separateness and symbiotic union.
Also, as one would suspect, the babies in Mahler's study often differ

dramatically in their developmental inclinations and capacities, but more of that later.

SEPARATION UNDER WAY

What Mahler (1975, 53) calls the "first subphase" of "differentiation" occurs "at the peak of symbiosis" when the infant is about six months old. During his more frequent periods of wakefulness the field of his attention gradually expands "through the coming into being of outwardly directed perceptual activity." No longer is the "symbiotic orbit" the exclusive focus of his limited, yet evolving "sensorium." In addition, the baby's attention gradually combines with "a growing store of memories of mother's comings and goings, of good and bad experiences" which comprise the mnemic core of what psychoanalysis calls the "good" and the "bad" object. The infant is more alert, more goal-directed, and his attendants begin to talk of his "hatching," of his emergence from the "autistic shell."

As the seventh month approaches, "there are definite signs that the baby is beginning to differentiate his own body" from that of his mother (Mahler 1975, 54). "Tentative experimentation at individuation" can be observed in such behavior as "pulling at the mother's hair, ears, or nose, putting food into the mother's mouth, and straining his body away from mother in order to have a better look at her, to scan her and the environment. This is in contrast to simply moulding into mother when held." The infant's growing visual and motor powers help him to "draw his body together" (55) and to commence the construction of his own separate ego on the basis of this bodily awareness and sensation. At times, the baby even begins to move away from the mother's enveloping arms, to resist the passive "lap babyhood" which marks the earliest months of life. As he does this, however, he constantly "checks back" to mother with his eyes. He is becoming interested in mother as "mother" and compares her with "other" people and things. He discovers what belongs and what does not belong to the mother's body–a brooch, eye glasses, a comb. He is starting to discriminate, in short, between the mother and all that which is different from or similar to her.

This incipient individuation on the baby's part is accompanied by considerable anxiety, the most striking manifestation of which occurs in the presence of strangers. Like so much else in the area of separation-union, "stranger anxiety" evinces two distinct yet interrelated aspects. On the one hand, strangers fascinate the infant who, in Mahler's words (1975, 56), shows great "eagerness to find out about them." On the other hand, strangers terrify the infant by reminding him of the other-than-mother world, the world of separation, the world that appears as symbiosis and dual-unity fade. After stating that babies vary in their susceptibility to stranger anxiety (and other anxiety as well), Mahler offers us the example of Peter who at eight months reacts initially with wonder and curiosity to a stranger's mild overtures for his attention; two minutes later, although he is close to his mother, even leaning against her leg, Peter bursts into tears as the stranger touches his hair (57). Such is the emotional turbulence that accompanies the onset of individuation during the first subphase.

INCREASING AUTONOMY, PERSISTENT AMBIVALENCE

Mahler divides the second subphase into the early practising period and the practising subphase proper. During the former, the ten to eleven-month infant becomes more and more deeply absorbed in his expanding mental and physical universe. He begins rapidly to distinguish his own body from his mother's, to actively establish a specific (as opposed to symbiotic) bond with her, and to indulge his autonomous, independent interests while in close proximity to her. In a word, he begins to *transfer* his absorption in mother to the world around him. He explores the objects in his vicinity–toys, bottles, blankets–with his eyes, hands, and mouth; his growing locomotor capacity widens his environment; not only does he have a "more active role in determining closeness and distance to mother," but the "modalities that up to now were used to explore the relatively familiar" suddenly transport him to a new reality. There is more to see, to hear, to touch (Mahler, 1975, 66).

Yet in all of this, Mahler (1975, 66) is careful to point out, the mother is "still the center of the child's universe." His experience of his "new world" is "subtly related" to *her*, and his excursions into the other-than-mother realm are often followed by periods of intense clinging and a refusal to separate. For an interval the baby is absorbed in some external object and seems oblivious to mother's presence; a moment later he jumps up and rushes to her side expressing his need for physical proximity. Again and again he displays a desire for "emotional refuelling" (69), that is to say, for a dose of maternal supplies–hugging, stroking, chatting–after a period of independent activity. What Mahler's children (and all children) want–and we come here to a crucial utterance–is to "move away independently" from the mother and, *at the same time*, to "remain connected" to her (70).

The practising subphase proper (eleven to fifteen months) marks the high point of the child's move toward a separate existence. Not only does he experience a dramatic spurt in cognitive development, he also achieves what Mahler (1975, 71) calls "the greatest step in human individuation," his upright locomotion. These "precious months" of increasing powers and skills comprise "the child's love affair with the world":

> the plane of his vision changes; . . . he finds unexpected and changing perspectives . . . The world is the junior toddler's oyster . . . Narcissism is at its peak . . . The chief characteristic of this period is the child's great narcissistic investment is his own functions, his own body, and the objectives of his expanding reality. (71)

Adding to the exhilaration, notes Mahler, is the child's "elated escape from fusion with, from engulfment by, mother." Here is the movement *away* in its most striking biological and psychological expression.

Yet even here, in the midst of this great expansion, this "love affair with the world," the paradoxical, ambivalent aspect of human development rears its head as mightily as ever in the form of deep-seated, pervasive anxiety. "The course of true love never did run smooth," observes Shakespeare, and the words would seem to apply to our earliest, developmental experiences. The child's rapidly expanding ego functions bring with them both the threat of "object loss" and the fear of being "reengulfed' by the mother. One minute he expresses a need for "checking back," for "emotional refuelling," for knowing exactly the mother's whereabouts; the next minute he forcibly removes himself from mother's caressing arms in an effort to assert his capacity for active, independent functioning. Sometimes the baby runs away to make sure mother *wants* to catch him up; yet when she does, he shows resentment at being held and stroked.

Even the enormous step of upright locomotion and the increase in perception that it brings to the child holds both sides of the dual-unity equation. It is the need for mother's emotional support at the instant he learns to walk that Mahler (1975, 73-74) captures unforgettably: "The child walks alone with his eyes fixed on his mother's face, not on the difficulties in his way . . . In the very same moment that he is emphasizing his need for her, he is proving that he can do without her." In this way, the toddler "feels the pull of separation from his mother at the same time he asserts his individuation. It is a *mixed* experience, the child demonstrating that he can and cannot do without, his mother" (73, my emphasis). As for the mother's *physical* absence during this period (she may be working, ill, etc.) it typically sparks sadness, or even depression in the infant. The "symbiotic mothering half" of the "self" is "missed" during the very subphase that is most obviously filled with the joys of separation (74).

UNDENIABLY ALONE

The entire separation-individuation process culminates at approximately thirty months in what Mahler (1975, 78) terms "the rapprochement subphase," the period during which the infant perceives with growing clarity and certainty that he and mother are separate beings, that the old symbiosis and the narcissistic gratifications (including omnipotence) that go with it are illusory, that he is physically and psychically *alone*. Here is Mahler's (78) powerful description of this watershed in a person's life:

> With the acquisition of primitive skills and perceptual cognitive faculties there has been an increasingly clear differentiation, a separation, between the intrapsychic representation of the object and the self-representation. At the very height of mastery, toward the end of the practising period, it had already begun to dawn on the junior toddler that the world is *not* his oyster, that he must cope with it more or less on his own, very often as a relatively helpless, small, and separate individual, unable to command relief or assistance merely by feeling the need for it or by giving voice to that need (omnipotence).

We may note parenthetically at this juncture that much magical and religious activity is designed to *deny* precisely this momentous event, and not only deny it but bring about its *reversal* through just those mechanisms that Mahler mentions here, namely "mere feeling" (wishing) and "giving voice" (prayers and invocations). During the course of the next chapter, we will explore these denials and reversals in relation specifically to Jung's alchemical interests.

With the erosion of symbiosis the "fear of losing the *love* of the object" (Mahler 1975, 78), as opposed to losing the object, makes itself felt increasingly in the child. Up to this point (the rapprochement subphase) the object and the self have been more or less psychically indistinguishable. Now, as differentiation occurs in earnest, the object's love becomes the focus of the child's attention. This does not mean that the original anxiety over loss of the object as part of the self disappears. It means only that an additional, more conscious or even cognitive anxiety has been superimposed upon the original, primal dread. Accordingly, the toddler begins to demand the mother's constant attention. He is deeply preoccupied with her whereabouts. He expresses enormous anger and anxiety at her leave-taking, and anguish at being left behind. He clings to mother, seeks her lap, and may begin to show a dependent interest in maternal substitutes. In a thousand ways he attempts to coerce the mother into fulfilling his wishes. He tries at times to be magnificently separate, omnipotent, rejecting: he will gain the mother's love and attention by showing her the proverbial "cold shoulder." At other times he plays the helpless baby. For weeks on end his wooing of mother alternates sharply with his expressions of resentment and outrage.

How do mothers react to all this? "Some cannot accept the child's demandingness; others are unable to face the child's gradual separation, the fact that the child can no longer be regarded as part of her" (Mahler 1975, 78). Yet, whatever the relational dynamics happen to be, they cannot stop the process (78):

> no matter how insistently the toddler tries to coerce the mother, she and he can no longer function effectively as a dual unit–that is to say, the child can no longer maintain his delusion of parental omnipotence, which he still at times expects will restore the symbiotic status quo.

The child must "gradually and painfully give up the delusion of his own grandeur, often by way of dramatic fights with mother–less so, it seemed to us, with father. This is the crossroads of what we term the rapprochment crisis" (79). Mahler observes in a sentence at which we prick up our ears as we near the study of synchronicity that "many uniquely human problems and dilemmas" which are "sometimes never completely resolved during the entire life cycle" have their origin here, during the end of symbiosis and the onset of separation (100).

RESOLVING THE DILEMMA

The resolution of the rapprochment crisis comes about in a variety of ways, the description of which concludes the first half of Mahler's study. As the child experiences a growing capacity to be alone, his clamoring for omnipotent control starts to diminish. He shows less separation anxiety, fewer alternating demands for closeness and autonomy. Not only does he begin to understand empathetically what his mother is going through, which allows him to "unify the good and bad objects into one whole representation" (Mahler 1975, 110), but he begins to identify with the problems and struggles of the youngsters around him. In this way, he begins to turn to other people, and in many instances to his own father, in his effort to satisfy his needs. And with the wholesale emergence of gender differences, he starts to participate in those activities that are peculiar to his/her sex.

Equally important, the child's capacity for verbalization and symbolization begins to lead him toward the cultural realm, toward an endless variety of substitutive or, in Winnicott's (1974, 118) famous expression, "transitional" objects which characteristically take the form of "blankies," storybooks, toys, pets, and so on, and which exist somewhere "between the child's fantasies and reality," in what Winnicott calls "transitional space." We might say that the child's growing ability to incorporate the world into his burgeoning ego leads him to a series of new internalizations, new inward presences, which are appropriate to his age and to the problems he confronts. He is beginning to live with his own thoughts and with the companions of his inner world. This is what we usually mean by "being alone."

In the majority of cases and generally for all normal children such developments culminate in the establishment of what Mahler (1975, 110) calls "object constancy," and with it, the inception of an individuated life. By "object constancy" Mahler has in mind "the presence of a reliable internal image that remains relatively stable irrespective of the state of instinctual need or inner discomfort. On the basis of this achievement, temporary separation can be lengthened and better tolerated" (110). This is the necessary step, the vital inward accomplishment, that permits further growth, further individuation, further ego strength in the pre-schooler and eventually in the school child.

Mahler devotes the second half of her treatise to several lengthy case histories in which we see children struggling from normal autism and symbiosis to separation and individuation. She strives in these sections to illustrate her theoretical position at the clinical level, the level from which the theoretical materials originally arose, of course. As she does this, Mahler makes clear something that she stresses in many places in Part One, namely that is the *combination* of a particular caretaker interacting with a particular child that ultimately shapes the child's emerging character in terms of both conscious and unconscious processes. Projections pass not only from the baby to the mother, but from the mother to the baby as well. "It seemed that the ability to cope with separateness, as well as with actual physical separation," declares Mahler (1975, 103),

> was dependent in each case on the history of the mother-child relationship, as well as on its present state. We found it hard to pinpoint just what it was in the individual cases that produced more anxiety in some and an ability to cope in others. Each child had established by this time his own characteristic ways of coping.

Thus, when we look at the whole picture, we spy an element of mystery, a unique, intangible quality that pertains to each mother-infant bond and that can never be fully explained by observers, or indeed by the mother and the infant who are involved in the relationship. What occurs early on is not strictly an enigma but it has an enigmatic aspect, and we must always bear this in mind. Human behavior finally escapes whatever logical space we try to fit it into. Reality *happens*, from the *inside*, and can never be perfectly reconstructed.

As I suggested in the context, the struggle for and against separation extends itself powerfully not only into the spiritual realm, but into the nature and development of our perceptual lives generally, including the whole of culture. Although it may appear a bit strange to express the matter thus, our ordinary consciousness in the widest, most all-inclusive sense is inextricably bound up with the early struggle over separation *and cannot be grasped apart from it.* We must remember as we move through the next few pages that what Mahler describes in the final paragraphs of her theoretical section is the passing of the rapprochement crisis, not the passing of the separation-union conflict. Indeed, it is the thesis of this book, and has been from the outset, that this conflict never ceases, that it so forcefully shapes and directs our conduct as to gain a place among the central conflicts of our experience as a form of life.

As Mahler (1975, 115) herself makes clear, a "sound image" of the maternal figure does not mean that the old longing for merger stops, that the fear of re-engulfment goes away, that anxiety, ambivalence, and splitting suddenly vanish, along with feelings of omnipotence and narcissistic grandiosity; it does not mean that the primal terrors of rejection and loss miraculously disappear forever. The establishment of a sound maternal image simply means that the little person can stumble ahead *still loaded* with the great, absorbing issues of the early time, still loaded with the stress that attends the erosion of symbiosis, still wishing contradictorily for both merger and differentiation, still smarting from the collapse of dual-unity. What occurs as the infant undergoes separation has been described by Dr. Ana-Maria Rizzuto (1979, 49) as a "life-long mourning process that triggers an endless search for replacement." To express the matter from a different yet crucially related angle, the passing of the rapprochement crisis simply means that one is now in a position to act-out among others this basic human dilemma, this rooted, unconscious issue as it manifests itself projectively at the levels of both individual and group conduct. It means that one can now seek for omnipotence, fusion, and narcissistic gratification in the wider world. In a manner of speaking, one is loose. The old cliché that we are all more or less neurotic hopefully emerges with fresh clarity at this juncture.

Let us deepen and enrich Mahler's findings, then, and conclude our psychoanalytic investigation of origins, by concentrating once more on the first years of life, this time with evoked companions, attunement, and transformation as the focus.

EVOKED COMPANIONS, ATTUNEMENT, TRANSFORMATION

The genesis and the formation of the self derive from the baby's initial mirroring experience with the mother. For the past few decades this remarkable aspect of our origins has been studied intensively and has come to be regarded as a central feature of our development. The investigations of Rene Spitz (1965, 81) and his associates during the 1950's and 1960's established at the clinical level the baby's inclination to concentrate on the mother's face–and in particular on her eyes–during periods of feeding. For three, or perhaps four months the nursing infant does not look at the mother's breast (or at the bottle held close to her breast) but at her face. "From the moment the mother comes into the room to the end of nursing he stares at her face." What is especially interesting in this regard is the connection between such primal gazing and the mouth, or "oral cavity."

While the child takes into his mouth and body his physical nourishment, he takes into his dawning awareness or his "visceral brain" the emotional, psychological materials that he discovers in the face, eyes, and bodily attitude of the mother. It is often remarked that the first ego is a body ego and that our later life is influenced at the perceptual level by the foundational experiences our bodies undergo as consciousness awakens. We have here a compelling instance of how this works. When Spitz calls the "oral cavity" in its conjunction with the mother's body "the cradle of human perception," he reminds us that sucking in and spitting out are the first, the most basic, and the most persistent *perceptual* behaviors among humans. They underlie at the bodily level our subsequent rejections and acceptances, our subsequent negations and celebrations of experience.

Although Spitz established the baby's inclination to stare at the mother's face, notes H. M. Southwood (1973, 235-39), he did not state that mother and infant spend considerable time looking at each other, nor did he contend that such looking, along with the mother initiating the infant's facial expressions and sounds, provided the means for the baby to regard the mother's face and sounds as his own. An inborn tendency on the part of the infant prompts him to seek out his mother's gaze and to do so regularly and for extended periods. The mother, because of tendencies developed during the course of her relationship with her own mother, sets about exploiting this mutual face-gazing activity. As the eye to eye contact becomes frequent, and easily observed by the investigator, the mother's inclination to continually change her facial expression, as well as the quality of her vocalizing, emerges with striking clarity. Usually she smiles and nods and coos; sometimes in response to an infant frown she frowns. In virtually every instance the mother's facial and vocal behavior comprises an imitation of the baby's.

Thus, as the mother descends to the infant's level she provides him with a particular kind of human reflection. She does not simply give the baby back his own self; she reinforces a portion of the baby's behavior in comparison with another portion. She gives the baby back not merely a part of what he is doing but in addition something of her own. In individual development, "the precursor of the mirror is the mother's face" (Winnicott 1974, 130). The upshot may be stated as follows: the kind of behavior we connect with the ego or the perceptual apparatus derives in large measure from the behavior of the mother. Not only does she trigger the ego's formation, she determines the kind of stimuli to which the child will attend, including the stimuli that will eventually come through language.

EARLY EXCITEMENT, EARLY AFFECT

These social interactions must not be viewed as purely cognitive events. In the words of Daniel Stern (1985, 74-5), to whose *Interpersonal World of the Infant* I now turn, "they mainly involve affect and excitement" and become part of the infant's effort "to order the world by seeking invariants." When the pre-verbal, inward Representation of such Interaction becomes Generalized into what Stern calls a RIG, the infant's "sense of a core self" (90), or what we call the "ego" in the previous section, is well upon its developmental way. "Affects," writes Stern (89), "are excellent self-variants because of their relative fixity," which means, of course, that affects are a central part of mirroring. By creating a "continuity of experience" (90), and in particular a "continuity of *affective* experience" (93), the RIG provides the baby with the psychic, emotional foundation of his subsequent perceptual interactions with the world. As the Duke of Gloucester observes in Shakespeare's *King Lear*, we see the world "feelingly."

Thus mirroring in its early stages (we'll come to the later stages very soon) comprises for Stern (1985, 103) a "mediation" in which the caregiver "greatly influences the infant's sense of wonder and avidity for exploration." It is "only the feeling state" that belongs to the nascent self, that is a "self-invariant," and "merger experiences" become simply "a way of being with someone" (109). The infant lays down over and over again the memory of specific affective episodes; he/she develops RIGs; and he/she becomes susceptible to subsequent experiences which recall the foundational ones. Later affective exchanges *reactivate* the original exchanges; they "pack the wallop of the original lived experience in the form of an active memory" (110). This is the *essence* of the infant's affective world.

EVOKED COMPANIONS

Employing terminology that will help us enormously in understanding Jung's conception of synchronicity, Stern (1985, 116) calls these active memories "evoked companions" and suggests that they constitute what psychoanalysis usually refers to as internalized relationships. "For instance," Stern (113) writes in an effort to let us know exactly what he has in mind, "if a six-month-old, when alone, encounters a rattle and manages to grasp it and shake it so that it makes a sound, the initial pleasure may quickly become extreme delight and exuberance, expressed in smiling, vocalizing, and general body wriggling. The extreme delight and exuberance is not the only result of successful mastery, but also the historical result of similar past moments in the presence of a delight-and-exuberance-enhancing (regulating) other." It is partly a "social response," but in this instance it takes place in a "nonsocial situation." At such times, the original pleasure born of mastery acts as a "retrieval cue" and activates the RIG, resulting in an "imagined interaction with an evoked companion" which includes of course the "shared and mutually induced delight" about the mastery.

Equally crucial for our grasp of synchronicity is Stern's (1985, 116) observation that evoked companions "never disappear." They "lie dormant throughout life," and while they are always retrievable, "their degree of activation is variable" (116). He writes, "various evoked companions will be almost constant companions in everyday life. Is it not so for adults when they are not occupied with tasks? How much time each day do we spend in imagined interactions that are either memories, or the fantasied practice of upcoming events, or daydreams?" (118) Robert Rogers (1991, 41) comments on these materials, "the seemingly unaccountable experience by an adult of strong emotion, such as love or anger, as a response to a relatively trivial situation involving a comparative stranger might be accounted for by assuming that an 'evoked companion' has suddenly been mobilized, however unconsciously. Where else could all that affect come from?" Thus "attachment is the internalized representation of repetitive interactions with caregivers" (1991, 41). What is internalized in the earliest representations "is not simply the infant's own action, nor the environment's response, but the dynamic interplay between the two" (1991, 41). Can anyone fail to spy here the manner in which these citations touch upon, indeed mesh with, our earlier discussion of separation anxiety as presented in Mahler?

Many individual and group behaviors and beliefs, particularly those which occur in the religious or spiritual realm, are designed unconsciously to address the problem of separation (and/or other psychological problems) by offering practitioners experiences that *evoke companions*. Such experiences grant the *solace of companionship* to those who are struggling in the after-separation-world, those whose aloneness, self-alienation, or persistent separation anxiety prime them to respond to an unseen universe of powerful forces and beings to which they are ostensibly *connected*. Indeed, many of the figures at the heart of religious ritual (God the Father, the Son, Mary, Guardian Angels) and New Age beliefs and behaviors (visitors from past lives or outer space, shamanic guides, channeled entities including Jesus) may be regarded in significant measure as projective, psychological expressions, or complex, multi-layered symbolifications, of those longed-for, inward *companions* associated originally with the *dynamic affects* included in the dual-unity situation, the baby's delicious, regulating, invariant and *internalized* encounters with the care-giving figures of the early period.

AFFECT ATTUNEMENT

What Stern (1985, 124) calls "the next quantum leap in the sense of self" occurs when the infant discovers that he/she "has a mind and that other people have minds as well." Here we come to the first of two direct, foundational precursors of synchronistic happenings. At about nine months, infants come gradually upon "the momentous realization" that subjective experiences are "potentially shareable with someone else." The infant "must arrive at a theory not only of separate minds but of interface-able separate minds" (124). This is not, of course, a "theory" in the usual sense, but a "working notion that says something like, what is going on in my mind may be similar enough to what is going on in your mind that we can somehow communicate this without words and thereby experience intersubjectivity" (125). Now, intersubjective relatedness or the "new organizing subjective perspective about the self" is built upon a foundation of "core relatedness," the sharing of affective states. Stern dubs this empathetic responsiveness between caregiver and child "affect attunement," observing that it comprises what is meant when clinicians speak of parental mirroring (138).

After presenting a wealth of clinical evidence for the existence of affect attunement, Stern (1985, 139) observes in a crucial passage:

> strict imitation alone won't do ... The parent must be able to read the infant's feeling state from the infant's overt behavior, must perform some behavior that corresponds in some way to the infant's, and the infant must be able to read this parental response as having to do with his own original feeling.

Parent and infant are engaged in what we can term "telepathic" or "clairvoyant" exchanges; they manifest a kind of ESP in regard to affective states and affective wishes–what they *want* to happen as they interact on this intimate, feeling level. Stern (51) writes:

> infants ... appear to have an innate general capacity, which can be called *amodal* perception, to take information received in one sensory modality and somehow translate it into another sensory modality. We do not know how they accomplish this task. The information is probably not experienced as belonging to any one particular sensory mode. More likely it transcends mode or channel and exists in some supra-modal form ... It involves an encoding into a still mysterious, amodal representation.

And again, what "the infant experiences are not sights and sounds and touches and namable objects, but rather shapes, intensities, and temporal patterns–the more 'global' qualities of experience" (51). And finally, "the experience of finding a cross-modal match ... would feel like a correspondence or imbuing of present experience with something prior or familiar. Present experience would feel related in some way to experience from elsewhere" (52-3). Here we have a *realistic, psychological source* (through reactivation or unconscious memory) of what Jung considers to be the "paranormal level" upon which synchronistic events ostensibly transpire. Moreover–and perhaps of even greater importance–the essence of affect attunement between parent and child resides in its *synchronous nature*, in its happily *timed* interactive quality. Parent and offspring are *affectively in synch*. The parent knows intuitively, telepathically, clairvoyantly the affective meaning of the infant's signals, and the parent provides response in a *timely* fashion, magically echoing or mirroring the infant's inner world *as* the infant makes that world manifest. Conversely, the infant strives to engage the parent affectively *in time* to gratify his (the infant's) surging affect. Synchronous rapport, in short, is the pith of pre-verbal existence, and "transaction" takes place, says Stern (139), only when such "conditions" are met. Just as evoked companions never disappear, just as they lie dormant throughout life waiting to be activated, so affect attunements become *deeply internalized*, providing the emergent self with a foundational legacy of feeling that is sought over and over again in subsequent years. Indeed, it is "attuning" with "vitality" that permits us as humans to *be* with one another in the sense of "sharing likely inner experiences" on a continuous basis (157). Here is a memorable consequence: when we discover (or re-discover) an attunement, an evoked companion, an energetic, affective fix, we often feel *transformed*.

THE TRANSFORMATIONAL OBJECT

Guiding us toward the psychoanalytic heart of spiritual thinking, toward the essence of its interrelations with the early period, Christopher Bollas (1987, 13-14) observes in *The Shadow of the Object* that the infant's experience of his first object, "the mother," is fundamentally transformative in character:

> It is undeniable that as the infant's other self, the mother transforms the baby's internal and external environment ... [She] is less significant and identifiable as an object than as a process that is identified with cumulative internal and external transformations.

Just as evoked companionship and affect attunement never disappear, so this feature of early existence "lives on in certain forms of object-seeking in adult life." The object is sought for its "function as a signifier of transformation." The quest is not to possess the object but to "surrender to it as a medium that alters the self," that promises to "transform the self" (14). It is an old refrain: having met you, or found Jesus, or joined the party, or started meditating, *I'm changed.* In significant measure, and in psychoanalytic terms, the refrain translates into something like this: I've rediscovered (through a degree of emotional regression) the transformational essence of the early period, of dual-unity, of mirroring. My new connection reunites me with a transforming internalized caretaker and thus diminishes my sense of separation. I am restored to the before-separation-world.

This conception of the maternal figure as transformational is supported by the overriding fact that she regularly alters the baby's environment to meet his need; she "actually transforms his world" (Bollas 1987, 15). The infant identifies his own emerging capacities of motility, perception, and integration with the presence of the mother, and the failure of the

mother to provide a facilitating environment can result in the ego's collapse. With the infant's creation of the transitional object (upon which I'll
expand in a moment), the transformational process is "displaced from the
mother-environment, where it originated, into countless subjective objects." The transitional phase is "heir to the transformational period." Not
only can the infant play with the illusion of his omnipotence, he can
experience the "freedom of metaphor" (15).

        In a section titled, "the search for the transformational object in adult
life," Bollas (1987, 15) declares that psychoanalysis has failed to take
notice of the "wide-ranging collective search for an object that is identified
with the metamorphosis of the self." For example, in religions faith, when
a person believes in the deity's potential to transform the environment, he
"sustains the terms of the earliest object tie within a mythic structure."
Such knowledge is "symbiotic" (16), writes Bollas, touching implicitly on
the theme of separation in Mahler. It (the symbiotic knowledge) "coexists
alongside other forms of knowing." Aesthetic objects, too, frequently elicit
transformational response from the individual, who may feel a "deep
subjective rapport" with a painting, poem, song, symphony, or landscape
and experience "an uncanny fusion" with the item, an event which "re-
evokes an ego state that prevailed during early [pre-verbal] psychic life"
(16). Such occasions are "less noteworthy as transformational accomplishments" than they are for their "uncanny quality," the sense of being
reminded of something "never cognitively apprehended but existentially
known." They draw forth a sense of "fusion" which is the individual's
recollection of the transformational object. Thus, as *psychological categories*, transformation and separation are integrally related once again.

        As I just suggested and wish to reemphasize here, the search for
symbolic equivalents to the transformational object, and the experience
with which it is identified, continues throughout the life cycle. We develop
faith in a God whose absence is held ironically to be "as important a test of
man's being as his presence" (Bollas 1987, 17). We visit the theater, the
museum, the landscape of our choice, to "search for aesthetic experience."
We may imagine the self "as the transformational facilitator," and we may
invest ourselves with abilities to change the environment that are not only
"impossible" but, upon reflection, "embarrassing" (17). In such daydreams
the self as transformational object is somewhere in the future, and even
meditative planning about the future is often a "kind of psychic prayer for
the arrival of the transformational object," a "secular second coming" of a
relation experienced in the earliest period of life (17).

        How does such transformation *look* during the early period? What are
its phenomenological features? Here we reach the second direct, founda-

tional precursor to synchronistic happenings. If the infant is "distressed," writes Bollas (1987, 33), the "resolution of discomfort is achieved by the apparition-like presence of mother" *who arrives in a timely, synchronous manner* to remove the "distress." Not only is the "pain of hunger" transformed "by mother's milk" into an experience of "fullness," but the transformation is accomplished *synchronously, as* the hungry child makes his needs known. Bollas calls this a "primary transformation": emptiness, agony, and anger become fullness and contentment. Over and over again during life's initial stages–hundreds, indeed thousands of times–the parent and the infant are joined in such ministering, *synchronous* encounters. The baby is injured; the baby cries out. Then what happens? The parent appears "synchronistically" to soothe and "make better." The baby is wet and uncomfortable; the baby starts to squall. Then what happens? The parent appears with dry garments and ministering hands. Stephen Mitchell (1988, 31), relying on Winnicott, puts the matter this way: the "key feature" of the "facilitating environment" provided by "the mother" is "her effort to shape the environment around the child's wishes, to intuit what the child wants and provide it. The infant's experience is one of *scarcely missing a beat between desire and satisfaction,* between the wish for the breast and its appearance, for example. The infant naturally assumes that his wishes produce the object of desire, that the breast, his blanket, in effect his entire world, is the product of his creation. The mother's provision and *perfect accommodation* to the infant's wish creates what Winnicott terms the moment of illusion," the "foundation upon which a healthy self develops" (my emphasis). In this way, the early period of maternal care comprises an endless series of "synchronicities." The big one, or as Jung would say, the "macrocosm," hovers over the little one, the "microcosm," and ministers to the little one's needs *just as they arise.* Eventually, as Bollas (4) points out in a passage that is also crucial to our purpose, the child starts to "transfer" onto himself the "maternal care system" by turning it into "the self care system," and he does this through what is perhaps the most important *internalization* of the early years, the internalization of the good object. Increasingly he responds "on his own," and in a *timely* fashion, to what he requires: food, drink, warmth, shelter. Thus he *begins to take care of himself.* The caregiver of infancy disappears from the external world only to re-appear in the child's internal world. As I have already suggested, however, the switch is never complete. As humans, we handle the separation from the caregiver through the creation of transitional objets, objects that often impel us toward the religious realm. Perceptually and emotionally, we deposit a residue of the parental figure at the ground of the environment in which we have our being. The upshot is obvious: the sacred and the spiritual are loaded with pre-verbal feelings of fusion and transformation, connection and change, union and the wondrous sense of the self's *alteration.* One is tied uncannily to an "other" who is numinous, *magical* because specific pre-verbal memories rooted in the dynamic unconscious awaken affects that "say so." The attainment of "grace" in its myriad, endless shapes and forms, and in its ultimate *mystery*, is the sharp reinfusion of the infantile transformational process into the life of the "changed" or "saved" individual.

Of particular fascination here is the close, even inextricable connection between maternal care and the development of the time sense. The essentials of the matter are captured in a seminal paper by Hartocollis (1974, 43):

> as tension rises and the mother is not yet there the 'good' object image or representation emerges protectively in fantasy and unites with the self-image in a need-fulfilling hallucinatory experience; but if the mother's arrival is further delayed, it begins to fade away rapidly. As the infant tries to hold onto it and unpleasure increases, the uncertain 'good' object begins to turn into a 'bad' one. It is the effort to hold onto the 'good' object and expel the 'bad' one that . . . creates the ability to anticipate the future.

Eventually what Hartocollis calls "object constancy" develops in the maturing child; the early hallucinatory process is replaced by the ability to anticipate the fulfillment of a need. As the fused 'good' and 'bad' maternal figures are set up within as the scaffolding for normal character development, a relatively trustful tendency to believe in good outcomes is projected onto the environment which begins to be experienced as continuous, as possessing the attribute of duration. Accordingly, the good object *is* in large measure *good time,* or *synchronous attention and care.* The bad object is, by contrast, delay and neglect. When we experience Jungian synchronicities in the now of our existence as adults, they are magical, powerful, "numinous" and convincing to the extent that they recall unconsciously the *timely ministrations* of the good, attentive parent. Indeed, Jungian synchronicities can occur in the first place only because people tend to compartmentalize or "split" the parental object into its "good" and "bad" components, and people *do* this precisely as a consequence of the *temporal side* of their early care. The *meaning* in a "meaningful coincidence" is, in part, the meaning that originates in good, timely parent-child interaction.

THE TIE TO THE CULTURE

As we saw in Mahler, the child's frantic efforts to resolve the rapprochement crisis culminate in his ability to create an entire symbolical universe and to have it inside himself in a space that Winnicott (1974) calls transitional–the word transition indicating the movement away from the caregiver and toward the wider world. In favorable circumstances or when mothering is "good enough" to prompt ordinary development, the child's potential space becomes filled with the products of his own creative imagination. If he is given the chance, the baby will begin to live creatively and to use actual objects to be creative into. If he is not given the chance then there is no area in which the baby may have play, or may have cultural experience; then there is no link with the cultural inheritance, and no contribution to the cultural pool.

Here is the process in some detail. The "good-enough mother" begins by adapting almost completely to the infant's needs. As time goes on, "she adapts less and less completely according to the infant's growing ability to deal with her failure through his own experience." If all goes well, the infant can actually gain from his frustration by developing his own idiosyncratic style of relative independence. What is essential is that the mother give the baby, through her good-enough care, "the illusion that there is an external reality that corresponds to the infant's own capacity to create." It is precisely within this area of creativity that the infant will begin to make his transition away from the maternal figure by choosing "transitional objects"–blankets, teddy bears, story books–which afford him the magical or illusory belief that he is moving toward, or staying with, the caretaker at the same time that he is moving away from her or giving her up. Such magic, such illusion, such creativity provides the child with his primary link to the "cultural realm," to the religious, artistic, and philosophic symbols that comprise the shared, illusory reality of grown-ups. In this way, there is a direct development from transitional concerns to playing, and from playing to shared playing, and from this to cultural experience (Winnicott 1974, 12).

On the one hand, then, our ability to make symbols, to imagine, to create, to use our powerful brains, is an innate ability that is nourished into production by maternal care. On the other hand, however, that ability is prodded into action by the very real problem of maternal separation. In the development of symbolic thought, and in the perceptual style that arises from it, there is an element of that rooted anxiety which we have been describing all along. Thus Geza Roheim's famous contention that culture itself, at the deepest psychological level, is a way back to the parent, a symbolic connection to the early time, rings true. Thinking, says Roheim (1971, 131) is deeply rooted in the emotions, and between thinking and the emotions the mental image magically resides. It means *both* away from the object (separation accomplished) and back to the object (separation overcome). Civilization originates "in delayed infancy, and its function is security." It is a "huge network of more or less successful attempts to protect mankind against the danger of object-loss, the colossal efforts made by a baby who is afraid of being left alone in the dark." I would suggest that the life of ordinary consciousness in culture is not merely a dream but a projective dream, one that invariably projects the objects of the inner world upon the objects of the environment.

QUALIFICATIONS AND REAFFIRMATIONS

The question arises: does the generalized model that I have presented thus far apply to all children, in all families, in all cultures, in our rapidly changing world? My reply is as follows: no one will deny that children, mothers, fathers, and families vary considerably in regard to developmental tendencies and interrelational styles. Mahler herself is careful to point out again and again that quality of response and rate of maturation differ dramatically among her youthful subjects and that such difference is compounded by the uniqueness of each parent and each familial situation. Recently, Mary Ainsworth (1983) and her associates have confirmed that babies do not react uniformly to specifically the problem of physical separation. For some, the departure or the absence of the caretaker is far more traumatic than it is for others. As for reunion, some children are reluctant to "make up" for a lengthy period; others are happily in their parent's arms right away. Yet the separation-union conflict is there to one degree or another in all children, in all parents, in all families. We know babyhood and symbiosis at the beginning; later, we know individuation and relative autonomy. Mahler's "phases," and the issues that pertain to them, appear to be universal. As for Stern and Bollas, who can doubt that infants everywhere thrive on feelings of attunement and companionship, and on the transformations that accompany maternal care? Stern and Bollas are writing about "life" as we know it as humans.

Similar reflections may be brought to bear when Peter Neubauer (1985) informs us that the mother is not always the central presence during the early period, that our rapidly changing culture increasingly witnesses the father (and others) assuming a pivotal role. Undoubtedly this is so. But even here, where fathers or uncles or nannies or aunts are conspicuous, the issue of separation-union will still be crucial for the developing child.

Motivational dynamics may shift direction, yet the scheme that Mahler gives us will continue to disclose essential conflicts and provide a useful foundation. I am not denying that future decades may require wholesale reformulation; I am only suggesting that we should continue to make theories, based on our best evidence, while the world around us continues to change. What choice *have* we, after all? Were we to wait for change to stop so that we could begin to make theories, we would never make any theories.

With regard to cross-cultural issues, which we can only apprehend as formidable, we must remember, first, that Jungian spiritualism is primarily a Western phenomenon and thus very hospitable to Mahler's scheme, along with the expansion of it (Stern, Bollas) that we have undertaken in this chapter. Secondly, psychoanalytic studies of maturational problems among non-Western peoples reveal, on the one hand, the enormous differences at work in the world, and on the other, the ubiquity of the separation-union conflict.

East Indians, for example, struggle mightily to achieve a coherent, separate self amidst a consuming and often maddening network of familial ties and responsibilities (Roland 1988). The Japanese struggle similarly with the powerful demands of the work group, a conformist, authoritarian extension of the original family structure (Roland 1988). And the struggles of *both* these people are complicated and deepened by the arrival of Western, often American, ideas and attitudes. Yet for all the differences, which I do not for one minute propose to minimize, we still see the basic, core conflict over union and separation as it emerges from Mahler and as it may be cautiously extrapolated to the adolescents and adults of other societies. Indeed, this primal struggle exists worldwide and is perhaps best illustrated in Eli Sagan's (1985) study of various cultures each of which appears to be negotiating a stage of Mahler's scheme.

Maintaining that "the psyche is the paradigm for the development of culture and society," and following closely Mahler's depiction of psychic development, Sagan (1985, 363) views the human community as a whole passing from a) early kinship organizations rooted in the familial bond, to b) complex organizations based on chieftainship and comprising the first, wrenching move *away* from kinship, to c) monarchic and archaic civilizations (Egypt, China) based on the elaborate, hierarchical arrangements which ensure individual security through stable social order. Sagan writes,

> society may choose to resist . . . the drive toward development, but once
> advance is resolved upon, society is not free to take any direction . . . it
> wants. No primitive society develops into an archaic or classical civili-

zation. Every primitive society that embarks on a developmental journey becomes a complex society. The logic within this advance is not
primarily economic, or scientific, or even rational; ... it is primarily a
psychological logic. The stages in development from primitive to
chieftainship to early monarchies to complex monarchies to archaic
civilizations are projections and magnifications onto society as a whole
of stages in the development of the psyche. The journey of the psyche
through the various phases in the process of separation and individuation is recapitulated in social development.

As for the advanced, democratic society in which we exist today, it is "the
least dependent upon fundamental kinship ties of any political system ever
invented" (375). For Sagan, then, the developmental conflict described by
Mahler is not only ubiquitous for the individual but for the group as well;
the *world* struggles with problems of merger and separation, with the
clashing needs for cohesion and personal, independent expression. With
all of this in mind, I will offer the following explanation of synchronistic
events as an alternative to the Jungian view.

SYNCHRONICITY: A PSYCHOANALYTIC MODEL

The synchronistic event is rooted overwhelmingly in projection.
Specifically, the subject projects the internalized caregiver back out into
the environment where the caregiver originally resided during life's early
stages. The ego boundaries that came to separate the parent and the child
are, in the synchronistic moment, *dissolved*; the external world and the self
are, once again, *interlocked*. The remarkable coincidence that triggers the
projection (I am thinking here on Jung's beetle) is, to render it impressionistically, "not supposed to happen": the subject of the synchronistic
event has *already transferred to himself* the object's caregiving function.
He is now the one who watches over his existence. *He* is now the one who
intervenes in a *timely* fashion on his own behalf. The synchronistic happening turns all this around. It suggests—and here is the magical, uncanny,
"numinous" side of the business—that the caregiver is once more out there
in the universe, that the caregiver has somehow *returned* to meet the
subject's needs *when* they arise, in a *timely* manner, as was the case
exactly during the foundational years. This is the unconscious *meaning* in
the "meaningful coincidence," in the two events that are linked integrally
by *time*. In this way, a synchronicity comprises a *return of the repressed*,
an *upheaval* that cannot be rationally or logically explained. If the subject
is religious, if he has partially transferred the caregiving function to the
deity, then a synchronistic event may be subsumed under the category of

the *miraculous*, the category of *divine intervention*, or *sign*. The projective element will pass through the realm of the subject's illusory, transitional creations. Freud (1959, 19) notes that traumatic incidents from the past can be reactivated by disturbing incidents in the present. Slumbering mnemic residues awaken. Accordingly, a remarkable coincidence is a kind of trauma. It strikes the subject as unbelievable, astonishing, weird. It shocks him or "shakes him up." Think of the jolt Jung's patient gets when he shows her the beetle. What the shock of synchronicity *predicates* is precisely the loss of ego boundaries to which I referred a moment ago. One has the sense of falling back into the early period when the external world in the form of the object hovered over one and ministered to one's needs. Remember, during life's initial stages the parent *is* the entire universe to the child. In the midst of this wondrous, uncanny episode, one that is ultimately "inexplicable," the subject may also experience the symbiotic affect, indeed the *gratitude* and *worship*, that characterized his early interactions with the maternal figure upon whose love and care he entirely depended. As the subject projects all this into the world, the world undergoes a *wishful transformation*. Shedding its ordinary qualities, it becomes a place of intimacy, of bonding, of caring–a place of maternal holding and solicitude. In a word, the transformational, synchronistic moment offers the subject an opportunity to *re-attach* himself to creation, to be "reborn" in a state of security and thankfulness. Synchronicity is an instance of transitional behavior, behavior that ultimately restores the early period, with the early period's *good object* as the centerpiece, of course. Synchronicity marks a regression to the stage when two were one in perfectly timed and attuned symbiotic exchange.

Throughout antiquity (and still in some primitive societies today) people *sought for* synchronicities from *the gods* through prayers and rituals. As parental projections fashioned unconsciously to account for natural events, the gods were the source of life and death, abundance and dearth, creation and destruction. Moreover, their powers were directly associated with the element of *time*. One beseeched the gods for rain when rain was needed, for wind when wind was needed, for protection when protection was needed. And when the gods responded positively and thereby *mirrored* the good parent's behavior, one felt at home and secure in the world. Synchronicity is a partial, individualistic, small-scale version of such ancient spiritual belief and practice. One *registers* the coincidence of an external event with an inward aim of one's own, and one consequently believes "the gods" are on one's side. The unconscious, mnemic reactivation of the early period and the good object's care gives a boost to the ego, a boost to the *will*. One feels *lucky* as the gambler feels lucky when he is winning. One feels fortunate, blessed, in synch with creation. In the Jungian consulting room, as we will soon see, it is the *therapist* who sits in the seat of the god. It is the *therapist* who "controls the climate," *and who devises the synchronicities*, the "meaningful coincidences," that awaken the patient's capacity for wishful *illusion*, that convince the patient of the world's "numinous" involvement in his desires and activities. This is the *goal* of Jungian analysis: to cement the patient's spiritual attachment to the world, to give the patient a religious, spiritual outlook, to load the patient up with religious, spiritual feelings. Synchronicity is ultimately an *instrument* to accomplish precisely this "therapeutic" purpose.

Let's move on, now, to Jung and his followers.

NOTES

1. The term "object" is used customarily in psychoanalysis because the infant has yet to perceive the caretaker, usually the mother, as a separate, full-fledged *person* in the way we normally intend that term. "Object" is a psychoanalytic attempt to render the phenomenology of the infant's perception.

2. Mahler's postulation of a normal autistic phase in which the infant experiences and internalizes symbiotic merger with the mothering figure, and in particular Mahler's suggestion that we as adults can regress to this autism, and *know* it regressively, has stirred controversy of late. G.E. Zuriff (1992) has synthesized and summarized the literature, and I refer the reader to his paper cited in the reference section. Incidentally, Zuriff finds nothing objectionable in Mahler's postulation of primary autism, remarking (30) that it is not strictly speaking "empirical" yet retains its "scientific status" as a "theoretical postulate."

REFERENCES

Ainsworth, M. 1983. "Patterns of Infant-Mother Attachment." In *Human Development*, ed. D. Magnusson and V. Allen. New York: Academic Press.
Bollas, C. 1987. *The Shadow of the Object: Psychoanalysis of the Unthought-Known*. London: Free Association Books.
de Mause, L. 1982. *Foundations of Psychohistory*. New York: Creative Roots.
Freud, S. 1959. *Inhibitions, Symptoms, and Anxiety*, ed. J. Strachey. New York: Norton.
———. 1971. "The Unconscious." In *Collected Papers*, ed. J. Riviere, vol. 4, 98-136. London: Hogarth.
———. 1974. *The Ego and the Id*, ed. J. Riviere. London: Hogarth.
Hartocollis, P. 1974. "Origins of Time." *Psychoanalytic Quarterly*, 43: 243-61.

Mahler, M. 1968. *On Human Symbiosis and the Vicissitudes of Individuation.* New York: International Universities Press.

Mahler, M., Pine, F., and A. Bergman. 1975. *The Psychological Birth of the Human Infant.* New York: Basic Books.

Mitchell, S. 1988. *Relational Concepts in Psychoanalysis.* Cambridge, Mass.: Harvard University Press.

Neubauer, P. 1985. "Preoedipal Objects and Object Primacy." *The Psychoanalytic Study of the Child*, 40: 163-82.

Person, E. 1989. *Dreams of Love and Fateful Encounters.* London: Penguin.

Rizzuto, A. 1979. *The Birth of the Living God.* Chicago: University of Chicago Press.

Rogers, R. 1991. *Self and Other: Object Relations in Psychoanalysis and Literature.* New York: New York University Press.

Roheim, G. 1971. *The Origin and Function of Culture.* New York: Doubleday.

Roland, A. 1988. *In Search of Self in India and Japan.* Princeton: Princeton University Press.

Sagan, E. 1985. *At the Dawn of Tyranny.* New York: Knopf.

Schafer, R. 1968. *Aspects of Internalization.* New York: International Universities Press.

Southwood, H. 1973. "The Origin of Self Awareness and Ego Behavior." *International Journal of Psychoanalysis*, 54: 235-39.

Spitz, R. 1965. *The First Year of Life.* New York: International Universities Press.

Stern, D. 1985. *The Interpersonal World of the Infant.* New York: Basic Books.

Winnicott, D. 1974. *Playing and Reality.* London: Penguin.

Zuriff, G. 1992. "Theoretical Inference and the New Psychoanalytic Theories of Infancy." *Psychoanalytic Quarterly*, 61: 18-35.

3

Unpacking the Jungian Projections: A New Psychoanalytic Account of Synchronicity

SYNCHRONICITY'S FORERUNNERS

In the most general, all-encompassing sense of origination, where does synchronicity "come from"? What kind of universe, what kind of world, might be disposed to see the occurrence of synchronistic events? How can such incredible happenings transpire, at all? How can synchronicity *be,* in the first place? What is Jung's perspective on this? Where does he take us to explicate the matter? Jung (S,427)[1] begins by drawing our attention to the "godfather" of his "views" on synchronicity, namely Schopenhauer's "treatise" titled, *On the Apparent Design in the Fate of the Individual* which "deals with the 'simultaneity of the causally unconnected which we call *chance.*'" Here Schopenhauer illustrates the limitations of science, and in particular, the limitations of causality, in explaining the occurrence of "meaningful coincidence," or "meaningful cross-connection." Whatever it is that brings about such things, quotes Jung (428), "'it is something that surpasses our powers of comprehension, and can only be conceived as possible by virtue of the most wonderful pre-established harmony.'" Jung (428) goes on in his own words, "Schopenhauer thought and wrote at a time when causality held sovereign sway as a category *a priori* and had therefore to be dragged in to explain meaningful coincidence." Hence it is to Schopenhauer's "credit" that he returns us ideationally to "that still medievalistic age when the philosophizing mind believed it could make assertions beyond what could be empirically proved. It was an age of large views, which did not cry halt and think that the limits of nature had been reached just where the scientific road-builders had come to a temporary stop. Thus Schopenhauer, with true philosophical vision, opened up a field for reflection whose peculiar phenomenology he was not equipped to understand, though he outlined it more or less correctly" (429). Through concepts like "pre-established harmony," and "universal order coexisting with the causal one," and "elective affinity," and "mutual attraction of related objects," says Jung, we are carried in a direction that will enable us to grasp the kind of world in which synchronistic events may occur.

As it turns out, Schopenhauer's nineteenth-century treatise, and in particular its reliance on the notion of pre-established harmony, was largely inspired by the philosophical visions of Leibniz (ca 1700), visions to which Jung soon turns in his effort to develop the cosmic background to synchronicity. While it was Schopenhauer who set the wheels spinning for Jung by dwelling explicitly and at length on coincidence, it was Leibniz who created a full-fledged, complex view of the world that appealed to Jung's sense of formal integration, divine unity, symmetry, correspondence, concord–the numinous, spiritual order of things. Leibniz's ideas act in Jung as a kind of cynosure or magnet; they draw forth a wide variety of metaphorical materials (both ancient and modern, eastern and western) which Jung finds especially useful in explaining the origin of synchronistic happenings. Let's prick up our ears in earnest, for in these metaphors we may detect, if only in a preliminary way, the psychoanalytic meaning of Jung's elaborate, multisided projections.

Jung (S,492) observes that "the idea of a correlation between events and meaning" began to disappear from western thought toward the conclusion of the Renaissance as the scientific age got underway. Eventually the idea was "banished" altogether. Jung (498) goes on,

> such was the intellectual background when . . . Leibniz appeared with his idea of *pre-established harmony*, that is, an absolute synchronism of psychic and physical events. This theory finally petered out in the concept of 'psychophysical parallelism.' Leibniz's pre-established harmony and the above mentioned idea of Schopenhauer's that the unity of the primal cause produces a simultaneity and interrelationship of events not in themselves causally connected, are at bottom only a repetition of the old peripatetic view, with a modern deterministic coloring in the case of Schopenhauer and a partial replacement of causality by an antecedent order in the case of Leibniz.

Within Leibniz's metaphysical universe, Jung maintains (493), "it is not cognition," but, "as Leibniz so excellently calls it," a "'perceiving' which

... consists of images, of subjectless 'simulacra,'" that directs us toward the realm of "absolute knowledge." As it happens, and not surprisingly, Leibniz's "images" are "presumably the same as my [Jung's] archetypes, which can be shown to be formal factors in spontaneous fantasy products. Expressed in modern language, the microcosm which contains 'the images of all creation' would be the collective unconscious." Again within Leibniz's world, "soul" and "body" follow their "own laws," but not toward conflict and tension–on the contrary, toward an "accord" that arises "by virtue of the harmony pre-established among all substances," which are "representations of one and the same universe," the *unus mundus* of absolute integration (499). Jung is at pains to describe this Leibnizean place impressionistically; in doing so, he draws upon several authors (Pico, Agrippa, Philo, Hippocrates) from whom we get additional metaphorical materials crucial to our psychoanalytic purpose.

The universe of pre-established harmony, the universe from which synchronicity may emerge, is one in which "all things" are "bound" and "knit" together felicitously into "one frame." Within this "frame," those things in which the spirit of harmony is "powerful" have a tendency to "beget their like, in other words, to produce correspondences or meaningful coincidences" (S, 494). There is a "unity of all things" (491); "everything is naturally arranged" (491). As with the "parts of a living organism," there is a "sympathy of all things" (489-91); indeed–and we come now to an unforgettable figure–there is "*one common breathing . . . one flow . . . one great principle of nature, . . . being and non-being . . . together*" (490, my emphasis). In such a place, "there is no need for intellectual knowledge" (489). One grasps the essential nature of the *unus mundus* through a kind of intuitive comprehension, or as Leibniz says, a kind of intuitive "perceiving." One knows through one's "inner eye" and "inner ear" how to "pierce to the heart of things" (489). *One knows.* There is "an inborn perception," an "inborn knowledge in living organisms," which brings absolute certitude about. That Jung gives this vision an explicitly religious spin, one that leads ultimately to the religious archetype, is as plain as day. In the Leibnizean realm of pre-established harmony, "'all things are full of gods'" (493); all things express "'divine powers,'" and "'divine allurements'" (493). One feels the "teleological" nature of existence, the *purpose* that resides in every facet of creation (493). Indeed, one apprehends in Leibniz's world that "final causes," twist them how we will, postulate a *foreknowledge of some kind* (493), a foreknowledge that emerges from our experience with a certainty like that of an "'oracle'" (493). "Every kind of natural or living power in bodies" harbors "a certain 'divine similitude'" (498). "Heaven and earth" unite in a single entity, the "World Soul" (494-95).

All of this is faithfully reflected in Jung's followers, who also offer us significant metaphorical items–I mean significant from the psychoanalytic angle. "Leibniz's basic conception of the cosmos postulates a 'pre-established harmony' designed and maintained by God," writes Ira Progoff (1973, 68). He goes on, "in practice, however, God does not intervene. The meaning of the 'pre-established harmony' is . . . that the universe is to be understood as a vast pattern in which all the individual parts . . . are interrelated" (68). And then, "Leibniz considers both causality and teleology as partial principles whose operation is possible only because of the larger context that sustains them. 'The two realms . . . are in harmony, each with the other' . . . The body follows the principle of causality; the soul follows the principle of teleology" (73). This, Progoff (73) concludes, "has the greatest significance for the hypothesis of synchronicity." According to Combs and Holland (1990, 67-8), "the notion of meaningful correspondence between causally unrelated sequences of events goes back . . . to Schopenhauer . . . [and] Leibniz." Schopenhauer believed "that each individual life follows a pre-established pattern or fate," while Leibniz embraced "the alchemical idea that the human soul contains a mirror reflection of the entire cosmos in miniature . . . All such concepts point by implication to a state of unity." This "unity," Combs and Holland (68) maintain, is "familiar to mystical thought throughout the world." Here is Marie-Louise von Franz (1992, 189-90): "meaning was understood by Jung not as something partial–for example, the meaning of a sentence–but . . . as the meaningful coherence of being as a whole." In "antiquity," this "cosmic" integration was "understood as the 'sympathy of all things, . . . a flowing together, a breathing together.'" In the Renaissance, "Pico della Mirandola, Marsilio Ficino, Agrippa von Nettesheim, and others picked up this thread again . . . Leibniz's idea of a pre-established harmony–an acausal coordination of all things, especially of soul and body, established by God–appears against this background" (210-11). Along with "Arthur Schopenhauer," states von Franz (211), these thinkers comprise the "forerunners" to Jung's conception of synchronicity.

ONE WORLD, IN ACTUALITY

Only during the course of the early period, when the caregiver and the child form the primary symbiotic unit, do we *actually experience, actually and directly participate in*, a *single, whole world* whose features are predominantly those found in Leibniz, Schopenhauer, Jung, and Jung's followers. Moreover, only during the course of the early period with its all-encompassing, core dyadic relationship do we *actually experience and internalize* a *whole world* in which *coincidence* or *concurrence* is a *central, regular feature* of the environment. Over and over again, dozens of times each day, hundreds of times each month, thousands of times each year, the caregiving parent, the *mother* in the literal or generic sense of the term, fulfills the wishes and needs of the child–and not only fulfills them but does so in a *timely* fashion, *as* those wishes and needs emerge, *as* the child works to communicate his emotional and physical condition. The child is hungry; the child cries out. What happens then–not necessarily *at once* but often *at once* and very close to *at once* under normal, healthy circumstances? The caregiver *appears* to nourish and to soothe. The child is wet and uncomfortable; the child cries out. What happens then? The caregiver *appears* with dry garments and with ministering hands. The child is injured; the child cries out. What happens then? The caregiver *appears* to comfort and "make better." Consistently, diurnally, again and again and again, do we all *experience* these events *directly*, do we all *participate in* this "order," this "pattern," this "correspondence," this "regularity," this "meaning," this "interrelation of all things," for *in* this early "universe" the caregiver and the child *are* "all things" phenomenologically. Indeed, only during this period of our existence are *two* so powerfully united into *one* (dual-unity); only during this period are "all things" so *concentrated* into one mutually devoted pair–a single "solar system" with twin stars revolving around each other. The first months and years of life, in fact, are *little else besides* an unending series of meaningful coincidences or meaningful concurrences or meaningful cross-connections, an unending series, in Daniel Stern's (1985) terminology, of physical and emotional "attunements." The "pre-established harmony" of our *actual lives*, our *actual experience*, is simply nature's creation of the integrated mother-child unit through which the furtherance of the species' well-being, the furtherance of the species' *existence*, is more or less assured. It is adaptational necessity, biological, adaptational *cunning* in the service of the species' continuation that "pre-establishes" the only prefect or nearly perfect interrelational "harmony" we ever *actually know* on the planet. The mother with the babe nestled in her arms is the unconscious source of Leibniz's philosophical-theological visions; the attunement of caregiver and child, and the endless *concurrence* that arises *from* that attunement, is the unconscious source of Jung's synchronicity: as the astounding, magical, uncanny coincidence transpires, as it is *registered*, one wishfully projects the internalized caregiver into the external world; one wishfully restores the original caregiving arrangement; some one, some thing, some presence is watching over me again. The environment and the self *re-merge*. The uncanny coincidence, which "can't be figured out" and thus lulls the critical faculty to sleep, is one's *excuse* for re-arranging the world in accordance with one's infantile wishes.

Let's listen further to the descriptions and images we carefully included in the previous section as we develop these points, as we suggest the *human realities* that reside behind the metaphysical language. Remember, Jung (S, 489-95) presents these descriptions and images as features of the Leibnizean universe where synchronicities are apt to occur. My analyses apply *solely to that presentation*. The source of the world's pre-established harmony "surpasses our powers of comprehension" because we cannot see its infantile origins as they extend themselves through unconscious memory into the coincidences that strike us as miraculous in our grown-up, ordinary lives. We cannot perceive in an offhand, everyday fashion the workings of the unconscious mind as it wishfully recreates the past. When we find ourselves infused with a sense of "elective affinity" between objects we are merely projecting the delicious interconnectedness we experienced and deeply internalized during the course of our symbiotic interactions with the devoted caregiver. When Jung speaks of "a mutual attraction of related objects" in describing the Leibnizean cosmos he simply reflects the early time when such attraction is the order of the day, an order that continues with varying degrees of intensity for several years. It is during the early period that "soul" (affect) and "body" (physical need) follow their own "laws" toward an "accord" which arises "by virtue of the harmony pre-established," the "harmony" that produces the *one world,* the *unus mundus* of parent-child integration. Indeed, the *unus mundus* as it emerges in Jung and others is a perfect re-creation of the symbiotic past when "all things" are "knit" and "bound" together into "one frame," when things have a tendency to "beget their like," to "produce correspondences or meaningful coincidence" (attunements), when everything is "naturally" and "sympathetically" arranged as in the "parts of a living organism," for that is what child and caregiver comprise in their *organ relationship,* a *sympathetic, living organism,* a *two* that functions as a *one, one whole world,* an *unus mundus.* It is during the early period that we have "one common breathing . . . one flow [from the breast and from care generally] . . . one great principle of nature," the "principle" of *mothering.* And of course it is during the early period that everything is "teleological," purposeful, directed toward a vital, "pre-established" end–the newcomer's welfare and development, and the parent's inclination to minister and care. The *final cause* is a reflection of the *primal cause*, the cause of nurturance and survival. The "World Soul" is an imaginative, shimmering expression of the soulful, foundational unit of caregiver and offspring through which we all derive our precious, earthly being.

Just think about it for a moment. The notions of "pre-established harmony," and "one common breathing," and "*unus mundus*" do not come out of the blue, nor do the emotions we attach to them. Some realistic source, some actual, natural source must in some measure give rise to these ideas and feelings. As it turns out, there is only one period in our lives during the course of which our experience *actually reflects, actually approximates* the kind of world that is suggested by the expressions: pre-established harmony, one common breathing, *unus mundus*. Do we dare rule this period *out*? Do we dare ignore it as we strive to determine the significance of the Leibnizean cosmos? No one would even dream of maintaining that the ideas and feelings we associate with marriage, divorce, separation, family, love, death, and so forth do not arise in some measure from our early interactional experience, our early psychological internalizations. Everyone understands that marriage, divorce, love, and death reach all the way down to our foundations as people, to the inner infant, the "inner child," as the popular usage has it. Why should pre-established harmony and *unus mundus* and the related notion of *synchronicity* be exceptions? Why should the belief that God has created a perfectly "symmetrical" universe in which miraculous coincidences continually occur for our potential benefit be an exception? Surely when we emote over the idea that a supreme being is out there, and guiding us, we are to some extent at least re-experiencing a time when *this was the case*. Surely that makes perfect, even obvious sense. And surely there is *in that* a perfectly obvious psychological *cause* for the occurrence of synchronicities, which, according to Jung, do not *have* a cause.

Arthur Koestler (1972, 94) writes in *The Roots of Coincidence* that Jung's idea of synchronicity is but another expression of Platonism, an attempt to fashion a world of eternal form that stands in absolute, divine relation to our ordinary world of material objects. Following Whitehead, Koestler suggests that we have in this a case of "misplaced concreteness," a case of ascribing concrete existence to what is actually a mentalistic entity. But we can see from our psychoanalytic perspective the limitation of Koestler's view. While synchronicity and the Leibnizean cosmos out of which it arises *are* psychological projections, they are projections of an *actual, concrete relation*–the relation of caregiver and child that comprises the foundation of our lives, the emotional and physical dual-unity in which our very being is rooted. The relation of parent and newcomer, *what occurs between them*, is as real as reality gets, and synchronicity is a wishful expression *of* that concrete reality.

However, as I observed in the immediate context and throughout the

course of Chapter 2, the caregiver's response to the child's wishes and
needs is not always perfect, not always immediate in time and space nor
appropriate in emotional quality. The early period of our lives harbors a
bad as well as a *good* object. When the grown-up restores that period
through synchronicity he restores it in an *idealized* form. He re-arranges
the world in such a manner that only the *good* object is out there watching
over him again. He has known enough joyous attunement, enough joyous,
magical, soothing concurrence to arouse his nostalgia, to make him eager
to resurrect, and re-attach himself to, the Edenic aspect of his early years.
In this way, synchronicity involves *repression* and *splitting*. It plays down
the bad and it elevates the good. Leibniz's realm of pre-established harmony, divine similitude, elective affinity, and the general sympathetic
interaction of all things is one of the world's most striking examples of
such splitting, such repression, such *idealization*, as is of course Jung's
wholesale subscription to Leibniz's outlook. As everyone knows, Voltaire
saw through Leibniz's wishful visions almost immediately upon their
publication and penned his trenchant satire of *Candide* which mercilessly
mocks the belief that we live in the best of all possible worlds by presenting multiple examples of earthly misfortune and cruelty. Sometimes, when
I find myself dwelling on Leibniz's "pre-established harmony" and Jung's
enthusiastic endorsement of it through synchronicity, I also notice my
mind drifting off to the death camp at Auschwitz, or to the atomic oblit-
eration of Hiroshima. Pre-established harmony? Divine similitude? One
common breathing? Mutual attraction of related objects? *Unus mundus?* I
believe it makes perfect sense to suggest that *pre-established harmony*
equals *re-established infancy*. *That* is where Leibniz's cosmos comes
from, and Jung's theory of synchronicity too.

MONADS

Leibniz's world of pre-established harmony is, one might say, meta-
physically inhabited. Its residents are called monads, and Jung is vigorously interested in them, to further explain his theory of synchronicity of
course. If the reader has been feeling skeptical toward my presentation
thus far (I have the deepest respect for skepticism), he just might feel a tad
less skeptical after reading about monads. The dictionary defines them as
individual spiritual substances from which material properties are derived,
but the dictionary doesn't begin to capture the rich, living metaphors that
shine through Leibniz, Jung, and Jung's followers—especially Ira Progoff.
Here is the essential information: monads are *blind* or *"windowless."* They
do nothing but "mirror" the macrocosmic environment in which they float

about. Monads are round. As *microcosms,* they have the same significance as the mystical *rotundum*; indeed, *rotundum* in the alchemical tradition that leads to Leibniz *means* "monad." Finally, monads are sealed off from one another; they are isolated in their round, individual being. The pre-established harmony or universal accord they collectively manifest is accomplished not directly or intellectually but *sympathetically* through a certain *correspondence* that cannot be grasped from an everyday angle (and that strikes Jung as similar to the phenomenon of mental telepathy). This is what comes out of Leibniz's head as he makes up his theory of everything. This is what Jung asks us to accept as he works up his theory of synchronicity. Let's listen.

Jung writes in *On Synchronicity: An Acausal Connecting Principle,* "although the monads cannot influence one another directly because, as [Leibniz] says, they 'have no windows,' (relative abolition of causality!), they are so constituted that they are always in accord without having knowledge of one another. [Leibniz] conceives each monad to be a 'little world' or 'active indivisible mirror.' Not only is man a microcosm enclosing the whole in himself, but every ... monad is in effect such a microcosm. Each 'simple substance' has connections 'which express all the others.' It is 'a perpetual living mirror of the universe'" (S, 499). Jung goes on (500),

> in the monad ... alterations take place whose cause is the 'appetition.' 'The passing state which involves and represents a plurality within the unity or simple substance, is nothing other than what is called perception,' says Leibniz. Perception is the 'inner state of the monad representing external things,' and it must be distinguished from conscious apperception. 'For perception is unconscious.' Herein lay the great mistake of the Cartesians, 'that they took no account of perceptions which are not apperceived.' The perceptive faculty of the monad corresponds to the *knowledge*, and its appetitive faculty to the *will*, that is in God.

And then (500),

> it is clear from these quotations that besides the causal connection Leibniz postulates a complete pre-established parallelism of events both inside and outside the monad. The synchronicity principle thus becomes the absolute rule in all cases where an inner event occurs simultaneously with an outside one.

With the rise of the "physical sciences in the nineteenth century," Jung observes (501),

> the correspondence theory vanished completely from the surface, and the magical world of earlier ages seemed to have disappeared once and for all until, towards the end of the century, the founders of the Society for Psychical Research indirectly opened up the whole question again through their investigation of telepathic phenomena.

Indeed (502),

> synchronicity postulates a meaning which is *a priori* in relation to human consciousness and apparently exists outside man. Such an assumption is formed above all in the philosophy of Plato, which takes for granted the existence of transcendental images or models of empirical things, ... the forms ... whose reflections we see in the phenomenal world.

Finally, "by virtue of his microcosmic nature man is a son of the firmament or macrocosm ... In alchemy the microcosmos has the same significance as the *rotundum*, a favorite symbol since the time of Zosimos of Panopolis, which was also known as the Monad" (492). Jung has more to say about all this, but these citations get at the gist of his view.

Here are a few choice citations from Progoff (1973, 67-9) to complete the theoretical picture. "The main philosophical antecedents of Synchronicity," states Progoff, "are to be formed in sources far beyond rationality ... Leibniz's *Monadology* culminates the rich development of European alchemical thought and epitomizes the conception of man as a microcosmic expression of the macrocosm." Progoff continues, "each monad is closed off separate from all the others, as though it were hermetically sealed; for, as Leibniz says, 'the monads have no windows through which anything may come in or go out.' On the other hand, the monads reflect the larger pattern in themselves, so that each monad is 'a perpetual living mirror of the universe.'" Progoff then declares (70),

> the individual monads themselves are sensitive to the workings of the universe and of the other monads, but this sensitivity varies according to the nature of the monad. While the fact that the microcosm reflects all the world results in a perception *of* all things *by* all things, this perception is largely unconscious ... The knowledge that comes to the individual monad unconsciously Leibniz refers to as the 'small perceptions.' They are always present latently in the soul, but they become manifest in a variety of forms as the individual monad matures toward 'perfecti-

bility' and expands its relation with the universe. This basic conception is quite in accord with the view of the self that Jung has developed so that, looked at from one point of view, we can say that Jung's psychology now begins to make possible the empirical documentation and modern practice of Leibniz's monadological view of man and the universe.

Jung and his followers often claim to be achieving an empirical support of their positions.

Think for a moment on Progoff's final words, on the whole "monadological view of man and the universe": could there be a more striking, unmistakable presentation of the early period of our lives, including the interuterine environment from which we emerge? Surely even the non-psychoanalytic reader will find himself unable to miss the massive, wholesale projection that is going on here. Leibniz and Jung and Progoff return us to the time when we *were* "windowless" and blind; when we *did* "mirror" the macrocosmic or maternal realm in which we existed; when we *were* sealed off, in Progoff's unforgettable phrase, "hermetically" from the world–little ones, *microcosms*, floating about in our infantile state. We are returned by these imagistic materials to a time when we *were* disposed, even obliged, to communicate "unconsciously" with other beings, and in particular of course with the caregiver; when we *did* perceive things "inwardly" in a manner that led to our *internalizations* and *unconscious projections*; when we *did* inhabit a universe of *correspondence* and *concurrence*; when we *were* dependent upon the mother's registration of our mirrored responses; when we *did* grow and develop through the *mutual mirroring* we enjoyed in the *mirror relationship*. The *rotundum* here is the *belly* or *breast* and the shape of the baby *in it* or *at it:* the *body* is the seat of the metaphor. The "hermetic seal" is the *autistic shell* from which the infant and very young child have yet to emerge (Mahler). The "telepathy" discovered by the Society for Psychical Research, the "telepathy" that in Jung's view resuscitates Leibniz's alchemical *weltanschauung*, is the "telepathic" communication of mother and child, the "wavelength" that joins them in attunement and empathy (Stern). Even Jung's followers are prone to pick this up. "Telepathic events usually occur between two people who have a deeply felt bond–between parent and child," writes Jean Bolen (1982, 32-3).

Jung returns us to the world of infancy because that is where we need to *be* in order to buy into synchronicity, into the projection of the caretaker, into the reconstitution of the umbilical tie to an environment that is first represented *by* the caretaker. This is the symbiotic picture of the

universe that will help us to accept the supernatural significance of synchronistic events. This, in short, is the *regressive prerequisite* to Jung's
theory. As Progoff (1973, 67) says, Leibniz's writings are "far beyond
rationality." It is precisely rationality that we must leave behind if we are
to repossess the early period of our lives. For let us remember, *only* during
the early period does the "monadic" view of things *actually obtain*. Only
then are we *actually* the microcosms we discover metaphorically here.
Only then are we blind, unconscious, telepathic mirrors floating about the
macrocosmic *rotundum*. Progoff (70) declares that Jung moves Leibniz
toward an "empirical" verification, but the only empirical item here is the
one Jung (as usual) ignores, namely the early stage of human existence
which is *the source of the whole projection*. Jung *never looked* at infancy,
at childhood, at the time during which we *were* "living mirrors" and
"hermetically sealed" little ones. *Had* he looked he might have seen the
way in which projection arises in alchemy, in Leibniz, and in his own
patients. He might have grounded his idea of synchronicity in actual
human experience as opposed to medieval tracts and the *Monadology* of
Leibniz.

TAOISM

While Leibniz and the alchemists may be in command of Jung's
Western front, Lao Tzu and the Taoists are firmly in control of Jung's
Eastern front. "The rationalistic attitude of the West is not the only possible one and is not all-embracing," Jung writes (S, 485); "[it] is in many
ways a prejudice and a bias that ought perhaps to be corrected." He goes
on,

> the very much older civilization of the Chinese has always thought dif-
> ferently from us in this respect ... Only in astrology, alchemy, and the
> mantic procedures do we find no difference of principle between our at-
> titude and that of the Chinese.

Jung then proceeds to offer us a "description" of "one of the oldest and
most central ideas ... in Chinese philosophy," that of "Tao" (S, 486). He
draws this "description" directly from the writings of Lao Tzu, and he
offers it to us as a key "to the basic idea underlying meaningful coincidence," or synchronicity. I'll ask the reader to prick up his ears once
again–that is, from the standpoint of psychoanalytic understanding.

There is something formless yet complete
That existed before heaven and earth.
How still! How empty!
Dependent on nothing, unchanging,
All pervading, unfailing.
One may think of it as *the mother of all things under heaven.*
I do not know its name,
But I call it 'Meaning.'
If I had to give it a name, I should call it 'The Great.'
(S, 486, my emphasis)

Tao, Jung continues, "'covers the ten thousand things like a garment but does not claim to be master over them.'" In it, "the opposites 'cancel out in non-discrimination'" (487). Tao "points to something that corresponds to *the visible*," something "in the nature of an image;" to "the audible," something "in the nature of words;" to "*extension in space*," something "with a form." Yet "these three things are not clearly distinguished and definable [;] they are a non-spatial and non-temporal unity" (487). The Tao is "eternal but has no name;" it is "shadowy and dim" (488). The "'state in which ego and non-ego are no longer opposed'" is called "'the pivot of Tao; (488). With Tao, "the existence of things had not yet begun;" there were no "differences . . . in a sense, affirmation and negation had not yet begun" (489). The Tao "fills the emptiness," and can be known only when one "pierces to the heart of things" with his "inner eye" and "inner ear." In the West, Jung concludes (489), the Tao is captured in Hippocrates' notion of "'one common breathing'"–that striking, symbiotic metaphor on which we pondered in the previous section.

Surely what we have here is *just as revelational* as the monadic harmonies of Leibniz and his alchemical forebears. Indeed, we even have *the mother* explicitly equated with the all-producing, all-encompassing Tao: the unconscious meaning pokes through the descriptive surface to reveal itself to the light of consciousness. Shall we move briskly through the material, indicating the realistic source of the projections? It is the object of the early period who is *there* "before heaven and earth," that is, before the child begins to perceive the outside world, to create his external reality, to discriminate the subject from the object, the inside from the outside. It is the object of the early period who is "formless yet complete," that is, not yet clearly distinguishable as a *person* separate from the subject, yet *complete* in her caring ministrations, in her symbiotic partnership with the newcomer. How "still," how "empty," is our first perceptual world, yet how "full," how "great," how "meaningful" as we sense its inextricable connection to "the mother of all things." It is she who is "unchanging, unfailing, all-pervading;" it is she who is "dependent on nothing," and who infuses the neonate with sensations of power and effectuality. She does not have a "name," of course, but she does provide the child with warmth and comfort; she does "cover" him "like a garment," while at the same time she does not "master" him in a controlling, unhealthy way. In fusion with her, "ego and non-ego" still do not exist, "affirmation and negation" are as yet unborn in a cognitive, intellectual sense. "Shadowy and dim," the object of the early years is "visible," but only as an incipient "image;" she may be summoned, but not with "words" (pre-verbal stage); she is "extended in space" as a kind of "form" rather than as a fully differentiated being. There is a "unity" in her presence, which is to say, she induces a proto-integration that is based on the good-enough-mothering we take in, yet this "unity" is not fully temporal or spatial because time and space are still in the formative stages as Kantian "categories." And needless to say, she is "eternal," the eternal caregiver in whom our internalizations are already taking root, the immortal object of the inner realm who will be with us on the inside until the end, situated at the ground of our identity, including our *religious* identity as in this very material at which we are now looking. She "fills the emptiness" as we bond with her through our "inner eye and ear," that is, through our attunement and our empathy. This is the Tao, the Eastern version of Hippocrates' "one common breathing," the delicious psychological merger we know in the beginning and search for wishfully when the beginning starts to disappear into "opposites." As Jung says (S, 489), "when affirmation and negation come into being," the Tao "fades." If all this is a key to "the basic idea underlying meaningful coincidence," to repeat Jung's claim (488), then that "basic idea" must surely be a *direct, experiential* outgrowth of the *only* period during which the mother actually *is* "all things under heaven," including the endless *concurrence* that marks the first stage of our life. Jung's failure to explore infancy and childhood is as conspicuous here, in relation to the Tao, as it earlier was in relation to the monad.

The metaphorical projections of Jung's followers are especially rich and helpful when it comes to the analytic tenor of the Tao. "Although words cannot express fully . . . the essence of . . . the eternal Tao," writes Bolen (1982, 3), "words can transmit the idea." What "words" does Bolen choose? The Tao is "The Primal Unity and Source" as well as "the Cosmic Mother" (3). The "major Eastern religions are based on the . . . unity and interrelationship of all things," which Bolen describes as a "basic oneness" or an "interconnected cosmic web" (5). Thus we find *the mother* cited explicitly once again as descriptive of the Tao, and of the synchronicities that emanate (somehow) *from* the Tao. Bolen follows Jung very closely:

synchronicity is the "key" that "unlocks the door" to the "Eastern apperception of totality" (7). We also find in Bolen the Taoistic "interrelationship" and "unity" and "interconnectedness" that we *experience directly* during the primal years. Indeed, the religious idea of Tao is *rooted in* such interconnectedness and unity. What ties us to the object early on is what *inspires* the development of spiritual imagery later.

According to Peat (1987, 22), Jung first used the word "synchronicity" as a *synonym for Tao* during the course of a London lecture in 1934. In a subsequent passage at which we briefly glanced in Chapter 1, Peat claims the "wellspring" of "synchronicity" may be discovered when we psychologically "plunge" into the "symbols of the collective unconscious" (111).

> It is like descending a dark passageway through a rockface and emerging into an underground ocean in which all minds have their origin. Within this hidden realm can be found the rhythms of the whole universe and the generative power of all that is matter and mind.

Here we have not only a classic expression of the *oceanic feeling* Freud associated with mystical states, states that return the practitioner to the time of infantile fusion, we have as well the biologic "dark passageway" that leads to the symbiotic object. Peat (111) also gives us the "rhythms" of the early period, the rhythms in which caregiver and child *attune* themselves emotionally and physiologically to one another. Assuredly this is the "wellspring" of synchronicity, for synchronicity arises from a wishful reactivation of that attunement, that concurrence, that timely, mutual interaction which fulfills the child's needs and wishes "rhythmically" as (or very nearly as) those needs and wishes *arise*. The "rhythm" of caregiver and neonate is found again in the "cosmic rhythm" that is connected *projectively* with synchronistic events.

The Tao, Progoff (1973, 75) tells us, "corresponds to Leibniz's 'preestablished harmony,'" that is, to the *one time* in our experience when wish and need are *invariably* met by the external environment instead of ourselves. When Progoff (75) proceeds to observe that the world of the Tao is "attuned" in an entirely "interior way," we immediately grasp the observation's significance: it explicitly reflects the *actual, internalized* (or "interior") *attunement* that marks the early period and that subsequently becomes the *ground* of our belief in synchronicities. The universe wishfully succeeds to the caregiver's ministering role. Such notions as preestablished harmony, and Tao, and interior attunement, Progoff maintains (75), are "suitable" for moving us toward the "subtle medium" in which "synchronicity operates." And indeed they are, for that "subtle medium" is none other than *unconscious memory and wish*–the straightforward, actual causes of ostensibly "acausal" synchronistic occurrences. Progoff concludes this section of his discussion by declaring that synchronicity establishes the "presence" of the "macrocosm" in the "microcosm" (76). To render this projective, metaphoric notion into realistic psychoanalytic terms is to say that synchronicity returns us to the time during which the big one, the caregiver, infuses the little one, the newcomer, with sensations of loving care and guidance, to the time during which the whole universe is *there* primarily to meet our needs. Synchronicity as *wish* wants to know that time again.

As to the question, are all metaphorical references to nature or world or Tao as mother necessarily regressive, necessarily reflective of an unconscious, regressive wish to restore an earlier reality? Can not a grown-up person reasonably find in the idea of mother a model for his external environment? The answer is, of course one can use the image of the mother in an ego-syntonic, non-regressive way. But in *this context* of synchronicity, of *acausal* coincidence, of the suggestion that the external world is somehow benignly, attentively involved in one's affairs, how can the maternal references *not* express a regressive, wishful aim? Jung *uses* Tao and monad in the service of *his theory*. I'm not responsible for the ten thousand interpretations of the Tao.

BORDERS AND BOUNDARIES

Drawing on Hesiod and alluding to the mythic, paradisal age–the "original state of man"–Jungian analyst Edward Edinger (1972, 8) informs us that "people are in union with the gods. This represents the state of the ego that is as yet unborn, not yet separated from the womb of the unconscious and hence still partaking of the divine fullness and totality." Let us go to the heart of the matter at once: the unconscious aim of synchronicity, of the *belief* in synchronistic events, is to *restore* this "union" and thereby overcome the *post-paradisal* "separation" from the "divine," from the "fullness" and the "totality" of the *first relationship*. The Jungian preoccupation with *boundaries* and *borders*, a preoccupation that runs like a thick thread through the literature on synchronicity, derives ultimately from the press and urgency of precisely this unconscious aim, this unconscious *wish*. Like everything else pertaining to synchronicity, boundaries and borders are *projective metaphors* waiting to be unpacked along psychoanalytic lines.

The Tao from which synchronicities arise, writes Jung (following

Wilhelm), is a "'borderline conception lying at the extreme edge of the world of appearances' ... In it, 'the opposites cancel out in non-discrimination,'" in a "'non-spatial and non-temporal unity'" (S, 487). Synchronicity, states von Franz (1992, 187), occurs in that "fringe area" where "magic, religious miracles, and scientifically provable effects" are "all mixed up together." Science today tries to separate these items, but synchronicity give science the lie. It is an "archetypal" phenomenon. It "constellates the archetype" (189) and can only be grasped as an acausal event that attests to "the meaningful coherence of being as a whole." The "closest thing" to this "view," notes von Franz, is the "Tao" or "cosmic intelligence" (189). Asks F. David Peat (1987, 115), "what could be the objective side to an 'acausal correlation?'" The answer: "a pattern of internal and external experiences" that arises "out of an order that is common to both." Synchronicities "therefore have their origin in a ground that lies beyond the particular categories of knowledge and defies all attempts to *place boundaries* or erect *mental divisions* between particular areas of experience" (my emphasis). Synchronicities are "manifestations" of the "unknown ground" that "underlies" both "mind and matter" (115). Indeed, says Peat (174), mind and matter "are not fundamentally separate" but "emerge out of a common generative order" in which all things are "enfolded." We are close to the realm of synchronicity, claim Combs and Holland (1990, 84), when we are "at or near *boundaries*," for "synchronistic coincidences" are "*boundary* events" (my emphasis). They "manifest" as "transitions across the margin between psychological reality on the one hand and physical reality on the other." They "can be seen as translations into the material world of psychological actualities." We seem "most accessible" to synchronicities "when we ourselves" have developed the capacity "to soften the barriers between the conscious and the unconscious." Such "softening," Combs and Holland (93) conclude, transports us "across borders" to the mythic realm of "totality." This is sufficient to capture the metaphoric thread to which I referred a bit earlier.

The Jungian obsession with boundaries is ultimately an obsession with the dreaded state of separation from the object, the state which represents *being on one's own*, without an omnipotent presence "out there" to watch over one's unpredictable existence. There are no actual boundaries or borders behind the Jungian material. The whole effort is to stimulate a partial, emotional collapse of the *ego boundaries* that define the grown-up person, and through such a collapse to regain for the believer the union or totality which characterized the early period of his life. What is unconscious here is the regressive agenda. Let me put it another way. As we develop, as we grow psychologically, as we differentiate ourselves from the caregiver, as we become *our own* caregiver and provider, we *set* ego boundaries, or borders; indeed, growth and differentiation *are themselves* the capacity to provide and to care for the self. Such evolving self-provision and care are accompanied daily by an increasingly mature awareness that one is separate from the parent, separate and able to minister to his own needs and his own wishes. "You can do that on your own," says the good-enough mothering figure to the four-year-old; "you don't need mommy to tie your shoelaces anymore." The projective, boundary metaphor in the Jungian literature on synchronicity attests to the regressive wish to *break down* that differentiation, to dissolve that demarcating "line" of the ego's progressive development, to collapse the subject into the object, and restore the earlier situation. The boundary metaphor as it emerges in Jung, and von Franz, and Peat, and Combs, and Holland says longingly, the caretaker is still available; you're not alone; you're not separate; you're not entirely on your own; the former relation still exists. As we saw in Mahler, getting separate, getting autonomous, getting differentiated is one of life's most harrowing and difficult tasks, so great is our dependence on the object during the early time. For some individuals, getting separate is too harrowing, too difficult, and so they gravitate toward the tragic refuge of mental illness. For many individuals, perhaps the majority, getting separate is softened by *religious illusions* (Winnicott) of which synchronicity, of course, is one peculiar example. As Jung (S, 486) tells us, for the Jesuits the Tao (synchronicity's engenderer) is simply "God." Synchronicity collapses ego boundaries because synchronicity *must* do so if it is to attract those religious seekers who wish to believe the caregiver is still out there, who wish to believe the vast, endless universe still has a place in its heart for *them*. And synchronicity dresses itself up in pseudo-science and quantum quackery because, in a scientific age, it helps to make religious illusions scientifically respectable, if it is at all possible to do so. Jung loved the "fringe areas" (von Franz 1992, 187)–synchronicity, UFOs, archetypes, telepathy, and so forth–because the "fringe areas" were just sufficiently difficult and obscure to permit the application of rarified or fringy scientific ideas. The modern religious seeker rushes in, convinced that he is being "objective" about his fantastic, wishful beliefs. The "unity of matter and psyche" (von Franz 1992, 249) in which synchronicity is ostensibly rooted is ultimately the unity of *mater* and child, the tie we all had to *relinquish* in order to gain those ego boundaries which define the separated self. How ceaselessly and cleverly the unconscious invents strategies to return us to paradise, to the Eden of our original symbiosis. A *coincidence*, an external event which seems to favor us or acknowledge us, or in which we happen to find some sort of meaning, is extrapolated to declare: the universe knows you're there, and *cares*.

AFFECTIVE MAGIC

As he moves strategically from item to item in his attempt to explain synchronicity, Jung makes the point that "synchronistic happenings" are "dependent on affects," on powerful feelings, on the subject's having attained an ecstatic, even "magical" frame of mind (S, 448-49). Such affect, such feeling, such magical mentation is of course "empirically" grounded in "archetypes," in the collective unconscious, in "images" which "do not spring" from the subject's "own thinking" (449). Progoff (1973, 106) is in substantial, although not full agreement with this. Synchronicity, he writes, occurs at the "transpersonal" level and is triggered by "the archetype of magical effect." It requires an "attitude" of "intense hopefulness" on the part of the subject, a "factor of emotionality" that creates a "one-sidedness in the psyche" (125). Progoff goes on (125), "in the case of 'magic causality' the factor of emotionality does not remain objective. Even though the entire process takes place deep in the unconscious, an egoistic factor is involved and the 'will' attached to the emotional affect is thought to be purposive and causative in nature." There is a willful, personal wishing for something, in short. The "archetypal images" do not explain the matter entirely. von Franz (1992, 195) states simply that the "experience of meaning" in synchronicity is "not only a result of thought but also something connected with feeling." Let's look a little further into this.

Jung's connection of synchronicity to the realm of affective magic is inspired by Albertus Magnus, a medieval philosopher and alchemist who maintains that the individual who deliberately falls into a state of emotional excess can tap into a psychic power capable of altering the world around him. Jung quotes Albertus lavishly, and obviously regards what he has to say as a key to the nature of synchronistic events. As the reader peruses these incredible, unforgettable sentences he might bear in mind that Albertus derives his thesis from a tract on magic by an earlier alchemical writer, Avicenna: "'a certain power to alter things indwells in the human soul,'" cites Jung (S, 448),

> and subordinates the other things to her, particularly when she is swept into a great excess of love or hate or the like. When therefore the soul of a man falls into a great excess of any passion, it can be proved by experiment that it [the excess] binds things [magically] and alters them in the way it wants ... The emotionality of the human soul is the chief cause of all these things ... Everyone can influence everything magi-

cally if he falls into a great excess, and he must do it at that hour when
the excess befalls him.

As I have already indicated, Jung strives to put Magnus' work on an
"empirical" footing by discussing it in an archetypal context. He also
claims (S, 446) Magnus garners support from experiments (by Rhine) in
the area of ESP, experiments that ostensibly suggest the importance of
emotion in achieving non-ordinary powers of perception.

Do we have to puzzle here for more than ten seconds before bringing
such material into a realistic psychoanalytic focus? What Jung gives us
through Albertus is a crystal clear description of the *omnipotence of
thought*, the belief–firmly rooted in the infancy and childhood at which
Jung never bothered to look–that *wishing for something, willing something,* indeed *having a fit about something,* is actually going to bring that
something about. It is during the early period that one's "passions" and
"excesses," one's outbursts and uproars, one's rages and weepings, and all
the rest, *did* have the capacity to "alter" the world, to transform the environment in a self-satisfying way, to achieve in Progoff's (1973, 125)
terminology, the "egoistic" aim of one's "will." It is this *infantile residue*
precisely that underlies all magical behavior and belief. Through his use of
Albertus, Jung discloses for us the extent to which synchronicity is a
magical, wishful "happening," an event residing squarely in the realm of
regressive longing.

Malinowski (1982, 242) pointed out more than half a century ago that
magical acts, one and all, are "expressions of emotion," and more particularly, emotion bound up with the possession or the lack of power. Engaged
in a series of practical actions, an individual often comes to what Malinowski calls a "gap" (242). The hunter loses his quarry, the sailor his
breeze, the warrior his spear, or his strength. What does an individual do in
such a case, "setting aside all magic and ritual"? Whether he is savage or
civilized, in possession of magic or without it, his "nervous system and his
whole organism drive him to some substitute activity." He is possessed by
his idea of the desired end; he sees it and feels it. Hence, his "organism
reproduces the acts suggested by the anticipations of hope." The individual
who is swayed by "impotent fury" clenches his fists or imagines an attack
upon his enemy. The lover who aches for the unattainable object sees her
in visions or mentally addresses her. The disappointed hunter imagines the
prey in his trap. Such behaviors are natural responses to frustrating situations and are based on a "universal psycho-physiological mechanism."
They engender "extended expressions of emotion in act or word" which
allow the individual to "forecast the images of wished-for results," and by

doing that, to regain equilibrium and harmony with life (242). As for the connection between magic and the early period, Roheim (1955, 11-12) was among the first psychoanalysts to spy it, and like Malinowski he drew upon his anthropological work in making his observations. "Magic must be rooted in the child-mother situation," he writes, "because in the beginning the environment simply means the mother. Therefore, wishing or manifesting the wish is the proper way to deal with the environment." Roheim then goes on to say–and let us keep our eyes open for the "gap" we found in Malinowski–"the mother is not only known by the fact that she gratifies the wishes of the child. In truth, she would never be discovered were it not for the fact that there is a gap between desire and fulfillment." More specifically, "magic originates from the child's crying when he is abandoned and angry; it is not merely the expression of what actually takes place in the dual-unity situation, but is also a withdrawal of attachment from the object to the means by which the object is wooed, that is, from the mother to the word and back again to the mother." Thus it is "obvious," asserts Roheim (44), "that we grow up via magic." We "pass through the ... phases of organization, and concurrently our mastery of our own body and of the environment increases. This is our own 'magic,' and it is analogous in some ways to the invocation of his own 'luonto' (or nature) by the Finnish wizard" (44). In a series of key, summarizing sentences, Roheim states that "magic" is our "great reservoir of strength against frustration and defeat. Our first response to the frustrations of reality is magic, and without this belief in our specific ability or magic we cannot hold our own against the environment." The baby "does not know the limits of its power. It learns in time to recognize the parents as those who determine its fate, but in magic it denies this dependency. The ultimate denial of dependency comes from the all-powerful sorcerer who acts out the role which he once attributed to the projected images." While the "magical omnipotence fantasy of the child is a part of growing up, magic in the hands of an adult means a regression to an infantile fantasy" (45-46). Magic says in the end, I refuse to give up my desires.

As for the "infantile fantasy" involved in *wishful, magical synchronicity*, it is as plain as day. I am referring of course to the fantasy of *reconnection to the object*, the fantasy that says, something is out there, watching over me; I'm not alone; this coincidence proves the universe is with me, on my side, whispering its secrets to me, as to an *alchemist*. This is what the believer, in Progoff's (1973, 125) words again, is "hoping intensely" for in his "magical attitude." This is what his "psyche" has become "one-sided" about. As for the "hour" such a fantasy "befalls" one, to repeat Albertus' wonderful words, it can be *any* hour, any time the coincidence triggers the unconscious memory of the early time and thus prompts the subject wishfully to project the caregiver back out into the external world. One is sad, or alone, or unemployed, or anxious, or whatever–in need of a boost, in need of feeling special or "lucky" in the gambler's sense. Or one is simply disposed to magical thinking, prone to find a supernatural meaning in things. Then something unusual happens by way of coincidence and the feeling arises, the emotion arises, the affect arises, the *sense of connection* arises. One is back in the old relation when the external world *was* there for one, when the external world *was*, in Roheim's words, "the mother." One is *at the center again* because one is *wishing to be at the center* and *using an external event to validate the aim of one's wishing*. Such an experience, needless to say, provides a strong impetus to one's *will*. The world is on *my* side. I'm going to get out there and *do* things, *my way*. The tie to the parent re-established in synchronicity gives one's self-esteem an enormous lift. The little monad swells up with hope, with a belief in himself, with the conviction that the cosmos is somehow behind him. One is "alchemically" *changed, transformed*. The dull, leaden, heavy "soul" becomes light and golden. It is no *coincidence* that the alchemical tradition stands behind the "archetype of magical effect," for the alchemical tradition is *devoted* to transforming the world in accordance with its adherents' desires. The whole of alchemy is streaked with the omnipotence of thought. The whole of alchemy strives unconsciously to restore the early period when one *was* omnipotent and magical. Had Jung looked at infancy and childhood he might have seen the *regressive* side of alchemical activity.

WHAT ARCHETYPES DO

The archetype of magical effect is but one small part of the story, of course. To get at synchronicity's full, unconscious significance we must view it against the backdrop of Jung's whole archetypal world. We will derive from such a viewing not only an analytic understanding of synchronicity but an analytic understanding of archetypes as well. We will be able to see *their* unconscious meaning; we will be able to unpack and demystify *them*. That synchronicity is tied integrally to archetypes is indisputable. "Synchronicity" is "bound up with archetypes," writes Jung (S, 437) in *Synchronicity: An Acausal Connecting Principle*. And again, "meaningful coincidences" have "an archetypal foundation" (438). And still again, "synchronicity ... rests on the psychoid factors I call archetypes" (515). As for Jung's followers: synchronicities "depend on the activation of an archetypal pattern," states von Franz (1992, 299). "The activation of an archetype is what triggers a synchronistic occurrence," declare Combs and Holland (1990, 69). Archetypes are "the real foundation of [Jung's] theory of Synchronicity," maintains Progoff (1973, 79). I could cite a dozen more comments exactly like these. Now, to fathom the connection of archetypes to synchronistic events we must not ask solely or even primarily what archetypes *are*; we must ask also what archetypes *do*. We must proceed *operationally*. We must concentrate upon the *function* of these things, on how they manifest themselves in the individual's psychic life, on how they act upon or influence the person who experiences their power. Jung's archetypal tale is designed to *accomplish* something for the person who subscribes to it. It has a directional, purposive character. It is not so much a metaphysical or theoretical item as a potential *shaper* of the individual's attitude toward the universe, including of course his own existence and his own actions.

As we saw earlier in relation to Jung's philosophical alchemist, Albertus Magnus, archetypes evoke powerful feelings, powerful affects that reach down to the elemental, foundational level of our lives. "The archetypes," writes Jung (S, 436), "are formal factors responsible for the organization of unconscious psychic processes: they are 'patterns of behavior.' At the same time they have a 'specific charge' and develop numinous effects which express themselves as *affects*." It would be difficult to overestimate the force of archetypal emotions. Whatever archetypes are, whatever archetypes do, they are implacable, irresistible, unyielding. Jung declares in sentences which border suspiciously on demonology (ST, 66):

> the energy of an archetype is not at the disposal of the conscious mind ... The energy of an archetype communicates itself to the ego only when the latter has been influenced or gripped by an autonomous action of the archetype ... It is a psychological fact that an archetype can seize hold of the ego and even compel it to act as it–the archetype–wills.

As for the origin, the source, of these compelling entities, we have instinctual, genetic Nature itself: "it seems to me," states Jung (TEAP, 69),

> that their [i.e., archetypes] origin can only be explained by assuming them to be deposits of the constantly repeated experiences of humanity ... The archetype is a kind of readiness to produce over and over again the same or similar mythical ideas ... The archetypes are recurrent impressions made by subjective reactions.

Accordingly, "the archetype is pure, unvitiated nature" (NP, 210). This is not to say, of course, that the archetypes themselves are unperceivable or undetectable. By means of "active imagination"–a kind of intense, specialized introspection–we can, in Jung's words, "make the discovery of the archetype without sinking back into the unconscious sphere, which would only lead to blank unconsciousness" (NP, 211). However, we cannot "discover," or know, the archetypes *directly*; we can know them, or discover them only as they *manifest* themselves through images, or symbols, or mythic materials. The archetype *itself* is "irrepresentable" (NP, 213). We come now to several key ideas which may be said to contain the essence of Jung's archetypal psychology as a whole.

The images, or symbols, or materials that move us most effectively to the archetypal level assemble themselves into a *binary system*. On the one hand, we have archetypal items bound up with the *mother*, and on the other hand, we have archetypal items bound up with *God*. That God and the mother are profoundly, even inextricably related in Jung's scheme of things will emerge, I believe, as we go. Moreover, *in* that relation resides another vital reason for viewing synchronicity along naturalistic lines. "What are the most immediate archetypes," asks Jung (CT, 34) in *Civilization in Transition*? He replies, "the most immediate archetype is the primordial image of the mother: she is in every way the nearest and most powerful experience, and the one which occurs during the most impressionable period of man's life." Jung continues (35),

> since consciousness is as yet only poorly developed in childhood, one cannot speak of an 'individual' experience at all. On the contrary, the mother is an archetypal experience; she is experienced by the more or less unconscious child not as a definite, individual feminine personality but as *the* mother, an archetype charged with an immensity of possible meanings. As life proceeds the primordial image fades and is replaced by a conscious, relatively individual image, which is assumed to be the only mother image we have. But in the unconscious the mother always remains a powerful primordial image, coloring and even determining throughout life our relations to woman, to society, to the world of feeling and fact, yet in so subtle a way that, as a rule, there is no conscious perception of the process.

Nothing, literally nothing, escapes the mother's pervasive, unconscious influence: "the all-embracing womb of Mother Church is anything but a metaphor, and the same is true of Mother Earth, Mother Nature, and 'matter' in general" (CT, 35). The father is also present, of course–as a "dynamic principle," a primitive "God-image," and as the route to "the society of men" (CT, 36). Yet the father's significance in the overall picture pales in comparison with the mother's. It isn't even close: "the mother is the first world of the child and the last world of the adult. We are all wrapped as her children in the mantle of this great Isis," declares Jung poetically (ACV, 94). Yet he goes even further, so far in fact as to make the mother equivalent to the very *structure of the psyche* (ACV, 101-2):

> the psyche is a part of the inmost mystery of life, and it has its own peculiar structure and form like every other organism. Whether this psychic structure and its elements, the archetypes, ever 'originated' at all is a metaphysical question and therefore unanswerable. The structure is something given, the precondition that is found to be present in every case. And this is the *mother*, the matrix–the form into which all experience is poured.

Jung denies that "all those things which take the place" of the original maternal presence are "nothing but substitutes;" he also concedes, "nevertheless," that "something is lost" in "development." What is this "something," precisely? It is the "irreplaceable feeling of immediate oneness" (CT, 36). Taken together, these citations comprise an overwhelmingly powerful attestation not simply to the mother's influence in the individual's life, but to the mother's *urgent unconscious presence* in virtually *every* area, including the area of *attachment and loss*, the area which involves the "feeling of oneness."

The second great archetypal force in Jung's scheme is the world of religious imagery, including above all the image of the "mandala" in its endless, and "numinous" variations (SDP, 213). For Jung, religious images move us away from the realm of the "ego" to the realm of "transcendence" (SDP, 213). Their powerful effects permit us to surpass our ordinary, stultifying egocentricity. We find ourselves gravitating toward *the self*, toward *the archetype of the self*, a spiritual, godly "zone" represented most persuasively and unmistakably by the *mandala* (SPD, 224-25). Here, we are able to identify with a "preconscious wholeness," to discover the "spiritual totality" which allows us to emerge from our "dark night of the soul" into the "divine light" of self-integration (225). The "individuation process," claims Jung prophetically, "is . . . a border-line phenomenon which needs special conditions in order to become conscious. Perhaps it is the first step along a path of development to be trodden by the men of the future" (226). Indeed, one's "individuation" is the "coming-to-be of the self." It does "not shut one out from the world, but gathers the world to oneself" (226). The *imago Dei*, the archetype of the self, and the individuation process are all integrally *linked* in Jung. The mandala, in fact, gives expression to *the God within*. "Mandalas" are "symbols of order," of "totality," of the *"imago Dei,"* of "the God within us" *(A,* 31-2). The "God-image in man was not destroyed by the Fall," it was only "damaged," claims Jung pastorally (A, 36-8) in a passage dealing with the "dechristianization of our world" and the "Luciferian development of science." The "spiritual man" *is* still available to us (A, 39). As we discover the "archetype of wholeness" through our movement toward "the mandala," we can re-discover our own inward "God-image" (40). The "empirical findings of [Jung's] psychology" reveal "that there is an ever-present archetype of wholeness" in all of us. The "original state of oneness with the God-image" can be "restored" (40). (Recall here the child's loss of his original "oneness" with the mother.) Such restoration, according to Jung, "bridges the split" created by our "contradictory strivings" in the world (40). Yet Jung moves the discourse to still another level: to discover the religious archetype in our lives (through, say, the mandala) is to discover God *directly,* for God *is,* actually *is,* an *archetype.* "I say as a psychologist that God is an archetype," writes Jung (IRPPA, 14), who proceeds to add immediately that "psychology" is "the science of the soul." For after all, reasons Jung, if we have an archetype over here we must have its "imprinter" (14) over there, and who or what could be the archetype's imprinter but God? As for our "psychic structure," it too turns out to be inextricably tied to sacred images: the unbeliever, asserts Jung, the "man" who is so "stricken" that he cannot find his way to the world of the spirit, is not merely unable to experience "sacred images" as his "inmost possession," he is also unable to realize "their kinship with his psychic structure" (IRPPA, 16). (Recall here Jung's claim that our "psychic structure" is the "mother.") But Jung goes further still. Not only do archetypes turn out to be God, they also turn out to be God's *word*: "the archetypes of the unconscious can be shown empirically to be the equivalents of religious dogmas" (IRPPA, 17). I cannot think of a stranger use of the word empirical than this one.

It is of particular fascination to see all this in relation to Jung's claim that our psychic structure is embodied in the figure of the mother, and the source of the archetypal world to be traced directly to her. In one place (ACV) it is the mother who stands squarely behind the fundamentals, and in the other, as we have just seen (IRPPA), it is God. There is no need, however, to puzzle over this, to try to explain it away, to claim that Jung changed his mind, to offer biographical and/or historical addenda. The simple fact is, Jung connected the mother and God in his mind. Why? To answer that question is to come face to face with the essence of what archetypes *do,* not what they are, or mean, but what they *do.* Here are the relevant citations. The "archetypes of the collective unconscious," writes

Jung (ACV, 22), are "as wide as the world and open to all the world . . . There I am the object of every subject . . . *There I am utterly one with the world*" (my emphasis). Again, "whether he understands them or not, man must remain conscious of the world of the archetypes, because in it *he is still a part of nature and is connected with his roots*" (ACV, 93, my emphasis). And again, it is "only" through his experience of an archetypal, symbolic reality that "man . . . can find his way back to a world in which *he is no longer a stranger*" (ACV, 110, my emphasis). And still again, it is the "archetypal, primordial images" belonging to "all men" that have the "power" to "*lead the individual out of his isolation*" (AS, 301, my emphasis). Is not what archetypes *do* perfectly clear?

Archetypes *end separation*. They restore us to "oneness." They embed us in "nature." They re-establish our "roots." They terminate our "isolation," our sense of being "strangers" in the world. That is what archetypes *do*, and that is why Jung connected God and the mother in his thinking; that is why his archetypal speculations comprise a *binary system.* It is the problem of *attachment and loss*, the problem of *separation*, that is tied inextricably in Jung's work to *both* the mother and God–*just as it should be from a realistic angle*. It is the mother from whom we are originally, experientially separated; it is the mother who is taken from us developmentally by nature; it is the loss of the mother that ends our primal sense of "oneness" with the world. And it is the archetype of religion, the *imago Dei*, the mystical union with eternal form (mandala)–along with, perhaps, the "womb" of the "Church"–that *restores* us to our "roots," to precisely the "oneness" we *knew*, actually *knew*, before the "split"–the original *division* from the parent. Accordingly, to find the godhead is to *refind* the "source" into which our "experience" is "poured." Jung intertwines the two strands of archetypal meaning because they *are* intertwined in our experience, and it is our *experience* that Jung projectively expresses *in spite of himself.* Archetypes do not end separation in some cultural or cosmic sense alone. They end the early, basic, primal separation about which we all feel *anxious* (some more than others) and *in answer to which* we all seek for substitute objects, such as God and the Church and the world of eternal form.

Let's remember, we are dealing here with *affects*, powerful emotions that distinguish themselves from feelings precisely because they contain an *unconscious* element grounded in the interpersonal past. We are *not* dealing here with intellectual abstractions. If the loss of infantile "oneness" is so profound, so "irreplaceable," as Jung says it is; if the mother's influence is felt *unconsciously* in every aspect, every corner of existence, as Jung says it is; if "Mother Church" and "Mother Nature" and "Mother

Earth," and even "matter in general" *are* the mother in *more* than a "meta-phorical" sense, as Jung says they are; and if the archetypes of religion restore us *affectively* to our "oneness," to our "roots" in "nature," to our sense of "union" with the world around us, as Jung says they do, then how can the archetypes of religion be anything *other than* maternal surrogates (or "transitional objects") and the affects they arouse anything *other than* maternal re-bondings? Jung's train of psychological thought is simply too *directional*, too tight in its implications, to allow us to reach some other conclusion. Let's remember, also, that the symbol of the mandala, the heart of archetypal religious awareness, is explicitly connected in Jung (A, 264) with the Tao, the Leibnizean cosmos, the realm of pre-established har-mony. Thus it reflects, or *mirrors*, the one and only time in our lives when we *did actually know and massively internalize* union, merger, totality, "oneness." The "self" called forth by the mandala is the self that was originally *nurtured forth* by the good-enough mother, the "source," the "matrix," even "matter in general," and *not* merely in a "metaphorical" sense. Strange as it may appear at first glance, the mandala mirrors the *aesthetic* of maternal care (Bollas), the foundational regularity and order which most of us *experience* during the early time.

It might be wise to remember here as well that life's primal, mythic journey as Jung espies it from his masculine perspective (ST, 303-04) involves the hero breaking free of his emotional tie to the mother and finding his way to the world of eternal form in general and the symbol of the mandala in particular–*the self*. But the archetype of the self is, once again, equivalent to the Tao, the Leibnizean cosmos, the realm of pre-established harmony and divine interconnection. Jung moves us in an *affective circle*. He takes maternal union away only to give it back again *disguised*. And this is, of course, the *unconscious* aim of all religious thinking: to reunite the practitioner with the original caregiver whose "irreparable" loss is miraculously repaired. God as archetype is God as matrix and final bosom. As Jung renders it himself: "the mother is the first world of the child and the last world of the adult. We are all wrapped as her children in the mantle of this great Isis" (ACV, 94). Jung admits in one place that archetypes *are* projective (AS, 300), but he also suggests they projectively reflect the godhead (AS, 301). Had Jung *looked* at infancy and childhood, had he *observed* the way in which powerful separation anxiety leads creatively and substitutively to the world of religious symbols, he might have *seen* what human beings are actually *doing* in their actual *lives* instead of inventing a collective unconscious from his reading and then *applying* it to the adults in his consulting room. Others were involved in such direct observation of young people during the years in which Jung was active. Jung, however, chose to look *away*. He rejected the theory of substitutes without putting it to the test.

As for the connection of synchronicity to archetypes–our original problem–surely it is obvious at this juncture. Synchronicity is archetypal in nature because synchronicity *does* exactly what archetypes *do*. Synchronicity *ends separation*; it establishes a "oneness" with the world; it proves that we are psychically "rooted" in "matter" (mater), that "Mother Nature" watches over us, is "there," is "present." Synchronicity says we are not "strangers" in the universe; if we are feeling "isolated," then synchronicity terminates that feeling. Just as we project the object into the symbols of religion, so we project the object into the coincidence that underlies the synchronicity. The *unus mundus* is present in *both* cases. And indeed, Jung regarded synchronicity as the parapsychological *equivalent* of the *unus mundus*, the eternal, divine "pattern," or form (S, 518). Writes von Franz (1992, 218): "according to Jung, the mandala is the psychic equivalent and synchronistic phenomena are the parapsychological equivalent of the *unus mundus*." There is nothing mysterious or transcendent or occult going on here; there is no telepathy or ESP or clairvoyance; nor is there the uncanny paradoxicality of sub-atomic physics or Einsteinean relativity. There is simply human projection, wish, fantasy, affective longing for union and care as we *actually knew* union and care during the early period when mother and child were attuned in a world of magical, endless synchronicity. In spite of Jung's abstruse terminology, paranormal speculations, and elaborate extrapolations from the medieval, alchemical past, synchronicity boils down to precisely what it is in the popular literature: a wishful claim that the universe is providing, "Someone To Watch Over Me."

These brief citations from Jung's followers will help us to pin the matter down. The "archetype of the self," states Bolen (1982, 23), allows us to "experience inwardly" our "relationship to oneness, to the eternal Tao that connects everything outside of us to us." Where do the archetypes live, asks C. A. Meier (1986, 311)? And he replies, at the "unconscious" level, the level of "the earth, our mother, Mother Nature in its original condition." Edinger (1972, 104) maintains that the "discovery of the archetypal psyche" is "equivalent to the discovery of God." After "such an experience," he goes on, "man is no longer alone in his psyche." According to Progoff (1973, 83), "archetypal images in their multitude of social and historical forms draw human beings into connection with the primary, most pervasive processes of the universe." One "participates" in the "movements of the cosmos" from the perspective of an "exalted" individuality. So much for the connecting potential of archetypes in general. As for archetypal synchronicity in particular, it suggests, says Peat (1987, 3), that "all of nature" may be considered "a single organism" in which "each person" has "his or her own place." Synchronicity allows us to become a "part of this harmony." For von Franz (1992, 258), the synchronistic event has a "healing effect": it permits the individual to sense his "connection with the universal Meaning," with the "superintelligence" of the "cosmic mind." One is deeply moved in his "feelings" and "emotions" by such "illumination" and "absolute knowledge." The synchronistic moment, in Progoff's (1973, 128) view, allows the "individual microcosmic life" to connect itself with the "larger general pattern of the macrocosm." Synchronicity "helps us perceive the movement of life in the universe as that movement is reflected in the life of human beings" (149). It is the "coming together" of the "self" and the "universe." For Aziz (1990, 175), synchronicity comprises "a strict mirroring of inner and outer events" prompted by the "objectives of the constellated archetype." And finally, for Bolen (1982, 78), synchronicity implies "a demonstrable connection between our minds or emotions and the physical universe, . . . the Tao." Through synchronicity, "we are aware of being connected with the underlying pattern of oneness in the universe" (94). Synchronicity tells us we are "cared for and no longer isolated" (97). When we "feel synchronicity, we feel ourselves as part of the cosmic matrix . . . There is indeed a link between us all, between us and living things, between us and the universe" (103). Synchronistic events are "clues" to "the existence of an underlying connecting principle, . . . the invisible matrix, . . . the Tao, . . . the great mystery" (36). Synchronicity ties us to "the Cosmic Mother" (3). Clearly, the archetype as a *connecting* entity, and synchronicity as a *transitional* occurrence projectively linking the individual to the internalized caregiver, emerge as vividly from the writings of Jung's followers as from the work of Jung himself.

ARCHETYPES DEMYSTIFIED

Glancing back to the context of this book as a whole, I believe it is time to suggest that archetypes are internalized objects and the archetypal world (or "collective unconscious") the experiential, personal world of human internalization. The powerful *affects* we discover at the so-called archetypal level arise from our actual, emotive encounters with other human beings, the *people* we psychically internalize during the years in which we bring our deep instinctual cravings–for care, protection, and love–to the environment we happen to "inherit." There is no need to look *away* from this environment in determining our foundations, as Jung and his followers do. There is no need to embellish our origins with gods, and myths, and Platonic forms, and heavenly "clouds of glory" (Edinger 1972, 10). The *people* who constituted our interpersonal universe, the *people* with whom we bonded, or failed to, are *enough*–along with of course our genetic endowment. As we develop, as we begin to let go of these power-ful, all-encompassing parental figures, we take them inside of ourselves psychologically, we *internalize* them, we create an inner realm in which we may have them, *possess them,* for the remainder of our lives. Thus do they become, in Roy Schafer's (1968, Ch. 8) expression, "immortal." We have in this the basic defensive strategy, the basic defensive method, for moving both *away from* and *toward* the object *at the same time.* We have in this the foundational paradox, the foundational illusion or self-deception, the foundational "magic" through which we strive to commence our independence, our autonomy, our capacity to will and to act on our own–and to *be* alone "with ourselves," which *means* with the "evoked companion" (Stern) internalized "from" the object. Eventually, as we approach adolescence and adulthood, we suffuse the entire external world with the parental presence by subscribing to a religious viewpoint, by projectively spreading the object out into the environment as "God" while retaining our internalized version of the object on the inside. And we have in *this,* ultimately, a clear biological, evolutional technique for diminishing separation anxiety, for making the world psychologically safe, or *familiar,* as that word calls family to mind. An animal functions better when its level of stress is low, and for the human animal, *separation means stress.*

Jung saw and hated the rise of science and technology within his emerging modern culture. He heard Nietzsche's famous pronouncement that God is dead. He perceived the decline of traditional religion in the world around him, and felt it in his personal life where it was probably linked to both his rebellion against his pastor-father and the need to explain to himself his own uncommon spiritual experiences. Hence, through a complex emotional and intellectual process which is not our chief concern, he broke with Freud and went on to invent his religious domain of psychological archetypes. All of this is anything but a secret. As Charet (1993, 198) expresses the matter, "Jung wanted to baptize psycho-analysis and turn it into a religion," and he made this plain to Freud in the now famous letter of February 11, 1910 in which he, Jung, states that "religion can be replaced only by religion." Freud's response was simply, "you must not regard me as the founder of a religion" (see Charet 1993, 198). There is nothing *wrong* with this, of course–I mean, with Jung's wish to create a new religion. We all have our goals in life. Yet here, in *this* book, we must *analyze* Jung's religion; we must explore it along realistic psychological lines as we would *any other religion.* And when we *do* that we discover its *transitional* intent, its transitional essence, its aim of uniting the practitioner, through "archetypes," with the object of the inner realm. Can anyone *miss* it, miss the unconscious significance of Jung's (ACV, 22) claim that "man" is "utterly at one with the world" when he finds the archetypal level, or Edinger's (1972, 104) that the "discovery of the archetypal psyche" is "equivalent to the discovery of God," or Bolen's (1982, 23) that the "archetype connects us inwardly" to "everything outside of us"? Even in the writings of Winnicott and Mahler it would be difficult to discover more accurate descriptions of the internalized object's psychological purpose and effect. Is this simply a *coincidence*? I don't think so. What Jung sublimates projectively as he fashions his archetypal universe of gods and forms, Winnicott and Mahler report straightforwardly from their direct observation of children. Jung, remember, was too busy with his theories actually to study the formative years.

I am not the first by any means to point out the similarities between Jung's archetypes and internalized objects. What Jung calls "archetypal images," writes Anthony Storr (1973, 37-8) in his fine book, *C.G.Jung*, the "object-relations school of analysts refers to [as] internal objects." Storr goes on to say that such objects "are presumed to be images of parents and other significant figures derived from the infant's earliest experience, 'introjected,' that is, enshrined within the psyche, and influencing all his subsequent experience of actual people in the world . . . That these images exist as active factors in the human psyche is not in doubt. Anyone who has ever worked in a child-guidance clinic will have had the experience of interviewing a child, hearing his description of his mother, and wondering what terrible figure will follow the child into the consulting room. When she actually appears, she is as likely as not to be a mild, kindly, ordinary sort of person, quite remote from the child's fantasy picture of her." Storr then declares, in an unusual moment of misapprehension, that it "hardly seems to matter" whether such images are called "archetypes or internal objects" (38). But it does matter, very much in fact, and I want to press the point with some energy. To use "archetype" is potentially to bring into play the Jungian theoretical model, a model that looks *away* from infancy and childhood in developing its central features, a model that turns to gods and myths, to religious dogmas and alchemical lore, in *typing* the people with whom its professional adherents interact. To view things "archetypally" is to push extraneous, irrelevant materials between the individual and the determining forces of his actual experience. It is to deal with an ostensibly *genetic* set of inclinations rather than with an actual psychology that bears the impress of the *real people* who participated in the shaping of one's life. The negative result of such a procedure is considerable: one is unable to *see* and to *understand* the interactional nuances of his own development. One is unable to grasp the manner in which the actual, interrelational past led to the issues and the problems of the present. In a word, one never gets in touch with the psychological realities of his own existence. One is robbed not only of the opportunity to perceive *what actually happened to him* over the years, one is also robbed of the opportunity *to change* in a way that *matters*, that is *genuine*, that enables one to contact his real inner world as opposed to a host of archetypal speculations and "images." The archetypal lens is ultimately a lens of distortion.

The very regrettable tendencies of Jungian theory reveal themselves most vividly in the writings of Jean Bolen, particularly her books, *Goddesses in Everywoman* (1985) and *Gods in Everyman* (1990). Bolen, a Jungian analyst, urges her readers and presumably her patients to discover through introspection which archetypes are governing their lives and to contemplate behavioral strategies based directly upon this discovery. The whole idea brings *astrology* immediately to mind, along with the demonological overtones in certain of Jung's remarks on archetypal forces (ST, 66). "Learning about . . . Greek gods," writes Bolen (1990, 7),

> can help men understand better who or what is acting deep within their psyches. And women can learn to know men better by knowing which gods are acting in the significant men in their lives as well as by finding that a particular god may be part of their own psyches. Myths provide the possibility of an 'Aha!' insight.

Bolen (7) continues:

> Hermes, the Messenger God, was the communicator, trickster, guide of souls to the underworld, and the god of roads and boundaries. A man who embodies this archetype will find settling down difficult, because he responds to the lure of the open road and the next opportunity. Like quicksilver or mercury (his Roman name is Mercury), this man slips through the fingers of people who want to grasp or hold on to him.

One could be reading the description of a "Leo" or a "Pisces" or a "Scorpio" in the weekly astrological column. Are you a "Poseidon man," asks Bolen? Well, your need for intimacy was probably ignored during your early years (10). Were you a "Hades child"? Well, it is no surprise that you presently value your solitude. Were you a "Dionysian boy"? Well, your "natural gifts" were "undervalued" in the past and that may explain your current penchant for "psychedelic drugs" (12). Were you an "Ares youngster"? Well, that discloses why you volunteered to fight in Vietnam (12).

And so it goes. I can't help wondering why Bolen's books lack a front-piece depicting her in her office with a tall, shiny peaked hat on her head–a hat covered with "archetypal" drawings of the gods–and a map of ancient Greece pinned to the wall behind her. Admittedly, such pathetic simple-mindedness belongs in New Age coffeehouses and bookshops more than it belongs in sophisticated Jungian circles, but Bolen's books *do* in fact disclose the way Jungian psychology works. Their very simple-mindedness lets the truth fall starkly out. They reveal the inveterate Jungian tendency to impose extraneous mythic material on the subject's past and thereby to *conceal* what actually occurred there. Think again on Storr's (1973, 38) comment that it "hardly matters" whether we employ "archetype" or "internal object." The sooner we drop "archetype" once and for all the sooner we will emerge from the dark night of Jungian theory.

Yet there may be a vainglorious element at work here too. I mean, how *flattering* it is to think we go about carrying god-like tendencies in our genes. How flattering it is to link ourselves up with Zeus and Hera and Hermes and Dionysius as opposed to the imperfect, flesh-and-blood creatures of our actual past. Are not the deities of ancient Greece prefer-able to mom and dad? Are not the heights of Olympus more compelling than the backyard, with its dandelions and dogs and fly-filled summer afternoons? What a grand, noble tale we have in all this Jungian material. We are immortalized, deified, transformed, transfigured. Imagine a room full of Jungians with everyone finding "gods" and "goddesses" in every-one else. "You really are a Zeus, you know. Ah, but don't overlook the Hera in yourself, my dear!" Our creaturely beginnings–the contracting womb, the groaning mother-to-be, the sloppy, slippery baby–and our creaturely conclusion–the sagging flesh, the bony hands, the worn-out teeth, the emerging skull–all of this is effectively *masked* and *set aside*. What a triumph for the ego. What a narcissistic victory for the fragile self coping perforce with its separation and smallness in the world. Those who are drawn to Jung require something more remarkable, something more spectacular, something more "numinous" as Jung was fond of saying, than the interpersonal, interactional realities of our here-and-now creaturely existence. In the end, however, we have only ourselves, so it's better to look. Not only is there a strange and wonderful beauty in the backyard, and mom and dad, and the actual world we joyed and suffered in, but looking allows us to *grow*, to achieve genuine advancement as people. That's quite a prize, from where I'm standing at least.

ETERNAL TRANSFORMATION

Let's note another feature or two of synchronistic happenings with archetypes as objects fixed firmly in our minds. This will allow us further to determine which approach makes better sense. As I have stated all along, I am not attempting to refute Jung's theory (an impossible task given the nature of the subject) but to offer an alternative to it, an alternative that will allow us to view the whole business from an entirely natural-istic perspective. Synchronicity triggers *transformational* affects, the sensation of having been *changed* or *altered.* The transformational empha-sis is birthed in Jung's essay on synchronicity (S, 439), of course, where the famous beetle episode is given an explicitly transformational and archetypal significance by the master. As Combs and Holland (1990, 83) express it in a representative passage that captures the Jungian position, synchronicity transpires "at just that psychological nexus where transfor-mation occurs," where we are "changed." We "undergo a transformation into a different person–a symbolic death and rebirth." As to *why* this occurs, it is, needless to say, because the "psychological nexus" of the event is one at which we invariably "find the archetype." All of this is echoed in Peat (1987, 27): "synchronicities are associated with . . . trans-formation." They "activate" the archetypal energy "deep within the psyche." They spark "an internal restructuring," a "new alignment of forces" within the "personality." When one is on the verge of "transfor-mation," says Peat, "all of [one's] energies are focused" on the "final turn of a card," and synchronicities "are bound to occur." Peat rounds things out with a number of examples involving famous writers and celebrities.

Now, it is precisely the demystifying of archetypes into objects that will allow us to shed some realistic light on this material, to *see* it for what it is in straightforward, naturalistic terms. We recall, first, the overriding fact that during the early period the caregiver *actually transforms the child's existence over and over again*, several times each day, dozens of times each week, thousands of times each year. The nature of the early period is transformational at its essence. "It is undeniable," writes Bollas (1987, 13-14) in a passage to which we turned in Chapter 2, "that as the infant's other self, the mother transforms the baby's internal and external environment . . . [She] is less significant and identifiable as an object than as a process that is indentified with cumulative internal and external transformations." Just as evoked companionship and affect attunement never disappear, so this feature of early existence "lives on in certain forms of object seeking in adult life." The object is sought for its "function as a signifier of transformation." The quest is not to possess the object, but to "surrender to it as a medium that alters the self," that promises to "transform the self." This conception of the maternal figure as transformational, maintains Bollas (15), is supported by the basic fact that she regularly alters the child's environment to meet his needs; she "actually transforms his world." The infant identifies his own emerging capacities of motility, perception, and integration with the presence of the mother, and the failure of the mother to provide a facilitating environment can result in the ego's collapse. In a section titled, "The Search for the Transformational Object in Adult Life," Bollas (15) declares that psychoanalysis has failed to take notice of the "wide-ranging collective search for an object that is identified with the metamorphosis of the self." For example, in religious faith, when a person believes in the deity's potential to transform the environment, he "sustains the terms of the earliest object tie within a mythic structure." Such knowledge is "symbiotic," writes Bollas (16), touching implicitly on the theme of separation in Mahler. It speaks for something "never cognitively apprehended but existentially known." Of equal importance here is our second point, namely that the mother's transformational significance emerges in close association with the occurrence of affective attunements (Stern). When the mother meets the child's need, the child and the mother come *affectively together*. They interact *on the same affective wavelength*, in *harmony* with each other, *in synch* with each other, affectively and aesthetically complementing each other. Needless to say, this transformational attunement does not, indeed cannot, always arise from a temporal context of perfect simultaneity. Although the mother is attentive and available, she is sometimes also busy, or delayed, or preoccupied, not entirely "there," or not "there" when the child wishes her to be "there." But this only makes the transformational moment more pleasurable, more powerful, more memorable, more *affective* in its ultimate result. After waiting in frustration for a time the child registers the mother's appearance and undergoes her transforming ministrations. The mnemic potentiality of the event, and I mean by that the *unconscious* mnemic potentiality, is *enhanced* by its very imperfection.

As we have seen, synchronicity entails a projection of the object into the environment. Once again the caregiver is out there, watching over us, caring for us, attesting to our merged, symbiotic condition in the world. The uncanny coincidence is just odd enough, just strange enough, to trigger a reactivation, a wishful unconscious memory, a kind of deja vu, that returns us to the early period of our lives. Once emotively in contact with the object again, once positioned reactively and affectively within the early period by virtue of the perceived synchronicity, we feel *transformed*, altered, changed, renewed, *not* because some "archetype" has been "constellated" but because *transformation actually was* our most powerful, memorable, and pleasurable experience during the early years of our *actual existence*. Of course we feel transformed. The principle function of the object we *internalized* early on was to *transform us*, to do *exactly that*, to change our needful condition into one of satisfaction and security, over and over again, for *years*. How could we *not* feel "transformed"? We have rediscovered the transformational object of infancy and childhood within (as Bollas puts it) the "mythic structure" of Jungian psychology, but because we are *unconscious* of what has actually happened, because we cannot *see* the true psychological significance of the event, we describe it to ourselves, and perhaps to others, as "archetypal," numinous, divine, a manifestation of the unfathomable Tao, or some such obfuscatory item. The "symbolic death" (Combs and Holland 1990, 8) that accompanies our transformational synchronicity is the "death" of our separate, autonomous identity; the "rebirth" is the reawakening of our original attachment to the caregiver. In Jung's mystical scheme, as in all mystical thought and behavior, "death" is regressive merger and "rebirth" is simply infancy and childhood the second time around. Surely a real mother and a real child interacting with one another comprise a better explanation of synchronicity than a wondrous instantiation of Platonic forms through a corresponding constellation of quasi-genetical "archetypes."

Much the same reasoning may be brought to bear on the Jungian association of synchronicity and *eternity*, or the *eternal*. "We must regard ... synchronistic phenomena ... or causeless events," writes Jung (S, 518), "as *creative acts*, as the continuous creation of a pattern that exists from all eternity." There is a "timeless order," claims von Franz (1980, 99), from which "synchronistic events" emerge. Synchronicity "grows," according to Peat (1987, 230-31), out of the "eternal timeless instant that is pregnant with the potential for change." It manifests the "eternal rhythm," the eternal "order" and "harmony" of "nature." Synchronicity is integrally linked to the "archetypes of the collective unconscious," states Jacobi (1959, 64); as such, it manifests a "timeless and unlimited structure" or "order" that is powerfully contrastive with our "individual temporality." I will stop here, although I could easily cite two dozen similar passages.

As we saw in Chapter 2, our "individual temporality" or ordinary sense of time is born in close association to the ministrations of the caregiver, in close association to the "rhythms" of the early period. When our needs are met *in good time*, when our frustrations are relatively short-lived, we are positioned emotively and physically to enjoy the timeless bliss of affective attunement. We are one with the object, in synch with the object, satisfied, gratified, fulfilled, and the moment might wishfully "go on forever." If we are fortunate enough to experience such care on a regular basis during the early years, we will develop what psychoanalysis calls "object constancy," or the ability to anticipate happily the fulfillment of our needs. In a word, we will gain a relatively trustful tendency to believe in good outcomes, and we will project this on to the environment. *Duration* will become *perspective*; "time" and "the future" will emerge as mental "categories." By contrast, if our needs are not met in a timely fashion, if care is withheld or unavailable, if our frustration turns to rage or hopelessness, we will experience the other, "bad" side of life's first stage, the timelessness or endlessness of abandonment and loss. From exactly this experiential place arise our projective or "creative" human notions of hell, purgatory, limbo, *bad eternity*. Needless to say, such temporally negative episodes will take their toll on the developing personality. We are social to the roots, and that includes our sense of *time* in its various expressions, from endless bliss to endless devastation and misery.

Synchronicity is a matter of *timing,* of course. Events turn out to be *meaningfully* connected because they are juxtaposed in *time*, placed "side by side" in a manner that enhances our understanding or accords us an advantage. The universe is proving its involvement in our lives through its temporal, or timely, participation in our business. But the coincidence we note, the coincidence we experience, the coincidence that begets our attention and *affect*, is inexplicable, "acausal," remarkable, uncanny–so much so, in fact, that it triggers *reactivation*, triggers an unconscious return to the period in which the caregiver *was* actually out there hovering over our dependent little bodies. Now, *this is precisely the period in which time has yet to be fully born*; this is precisely the period in which goodness and badness *are* able to go on existentially *forever*; this is precisely the period in which we *do* know "eternity," "timelessness," the "eternal rhythms" of a universe which *is*, for the developing child, commensurate with the caregiver, with the one who is *actually watching over us*. Synchronicity is associated with "eternity" for the same reason it is associated with "transformation." It projectively restores the object, which means the object's affective features. As the old psychoanalytic expression has it, synchronicity involves a "return of the repressed." That synchronicities are overwhelmingly *good*, useful, constructive, positive, that we cannot find in the Jungian literature instances of the universe working *against* the subject, that pre-established harmony rather than pre-established disharmony is the wishful context out of which synchronicities arise, only underscores the extent to which the believer, or subscriber, has *split* his psychological world–in true Leibnizean or Panglossian fashion I might add. It is the *good* object with whom he regressively reunites. It is the good object with whom he regressively associates his sense of "eternal rhythms." What he once knew in experiential reality as a *child*, he would have again in regressive fantasy as a *grown-up*. Thus does magical thinking endeavor to vanquish *time*, to transform it into "eternity" by moving psychologically into the past, into the mother's realm.

BACK TO THE CONSULTING ROOM

We are just about ready, from a theoretical angle, to make our promised return to Jung's consulting room, to the analytic setting, to the doctor-patient relationship from which arises our most famous example of synchronicity, namely the one in which Jung presents a beetle to his astonished patient who has just had a dream about a beetle. All that remains by way of preparation is to spend a few moments considering the manner in which Jung understands the role of the *psychiatrist* in the modern world. With the decline of traditional religion, and with the rise of "atheism" and "materialism," life has become more and more "difficult" for the men and women of Western culture, writes Jung (CT 258). "This is because the religious impulse rests on an instinctive basis and is therefore a specifically human function. You can take away a man's gods, but only to give him others in return" (258). Indeed, "the individual who is not anchored in God can offer no resistance on his own resources to the physical and moral blandishments of the world" (258). This is where the psychiatrist comes in: "just as the neurotic, despite unconsciousness of his other side, has a dim premonition that all is not well with his psychic economy, so Western man has developed an instinctive interest in his psyche and in 'psychology.' Thus it is that the psychiatrist is summoned willy-nilly to appear on the world stage, and questions are addressed to him which . . . concern the most intimate and hidden life of the individual, but which in the last analysis are the direct effects of the Zeitgeist" (CT, 281). It is the psychiatrist, then, whom the Zeitgeist has chosen to *rescue* the godless individual, the "lonely, empty, modern man" (76), the "uprooted wraith" (76) who has "broken" with his "tradition" and thereby lost his dwelling place in the "maternal womb" of "common unconsciousness" (75). From the very "edge" of the modern world, from the very abyss of cultural "enstrangement" (75), *the psychiatrist* will pluck back his floundering clients.

Jung has no doubt about what his clients need. There is no question in his mind as to what is good for them. "Among all my patients in the second half of life–that is to say, over thirty-five," he writes (PR, par.509), "there has not been one whose problem in the last resort was not that of finding a religious outlook on life. It is safe to say that every one of them fell ill because he had lost what the living religions of every age have given to their followers, and none of them has really been healed who did not regain his religious outlook. This of course has nothing . . . to do with a particular creed or membership of a church." Thus, as Jung views them, his adult patient are "ill," are *sick* because they have lost their "living religion," and they will find "healing" *only* when they have managed to "regain" their "religious outlook." The psychiatrist's role in the modern world is beginning to emerge in earnest: it is that of a secular *priest*, a sacerdotal professional who guides his supplicants into the presence of the deity. As Jung states in his famous letter to Freud (Feb. 11, 1910), composed as he decides to leave the Vienna circle and go his own way, "religion can be replaced only by religion." As for Jung's religious *doctrine*, as for the restorative religious teaching he will offer his spiritually thirsty clientele, it is of course his whole psychology in general and his theory of the *archetype* in particular.

As we have already noted, the archetype for Jung *is* God, and the archetype of the self (represented by the mandala) the *God within* (A, 32). "I say as a psychologist that God is an archetype" (IRPPA, 14) and that "the spontaneous symbols of the self, or of wholeness, cannot in practice be distinguished from a God-image" (A, 40). To unearth the "archetype of wholeness" is to "restore" the individual to his "original state of oneness" with the deity (A, 40), to terminate his lostness, his alienation, his *sickness* as a "modern man," and it is precisely the psychiatrist's "aim" to accomplish this "restoration." The "therapist's aim," declares Jung (CT, 237), "is to bring the positive, valuable, and living quality of the archetype . . . into reality," to "integrate [it] into consciousness." However, the "therapist" does not go about this haphazardly; on the contrary, he has a particular *style*, a particular working *method* for fulfilling his newly discovered purpose, his newly discovered role on the "world stage." Jung gives us the essential information in *Aion* (A, 13): "in describing the living processes of the psyche, I deliberately and consciously give preference to a dramatic, mythological way of thinking and speaking, because this is not only more expressive but also more exact than an abstract scientific terminology." It is "affect," claims Jung (A, 33), that draws the individual toward the archetypal realm; "purely intellectual insight" (A, 33) will not do the job. One must "experience the thing from inside" (A, 33). Jung calls his "dramatic, mythological" style–which emanates from his "anima," incidentally–a "projection-making factor" (A, 13), that is to say, a "factor" that elicits projections from both the master and from those who are attentive to the master's teachings.

Let's return now to Jung's consulting room and carefully review the materials that pertain to the famous beetle. "A young woman I was treating," Jung writes (S, 438),

> had, at a critical moment, a dream in which she was given a golden scarab. While she was telling me this dream I sat with my back to the closed window. Suddenly I heard a noise behind me, like a gentle tapping. I turned around and saw a flying insect knocking against the window-pane from outside. I opened the window and caught the creature in the air as it flew in. It was the nearest analogy to a golden scarab that one finds in our latitudes, a scarabaeid beetle, the common rose-chafer . . . which contrary to its usual habits had evidently felt an urge to get into a dark room at this particular moment.

Jung regards the event as a "meaningful coincidence" and suggests that it has an "archetypal foundation" (439). Returning to his patient, he observes (439),

> it was an extraordinarily difficult case to treat, and up to the time of the dream little or no progress had been made. I should explain that the main reason for this was my patient's animus, which was steeped in Cartesian philosophy and clung so rigidly to its own idea of reality that the efforts of three doctors–I was the third–had not been able to weaken it. Evidently something quite irrational was needed which was beyond my powers to produce. The dream alone was enough to disturb ever so slightly the rationalistic attitude of my patient. But when the 'scarab' came flying in through the window in actual fact, her natural being could burst through the armor of her animus possession and the process of transformation could begin to move. Any essential change of attitude signifies a psychic renewal which is usually accompanied by symbols of rebirth in the patient's dreams and fantasies. The scarab is a classic example of a rebirth symbol. The ancient Egyptian Book of What Is in the Netherworld describes how the dead sun-god changes himself at the tenth station into Khepri, the scarab, and then, at the twelfth station, mounts the barge which carries the rejuvenated sun-god into the morning sky.

Jung concludes with the following remarks (440-41):

> The patient with the scarab found herself in an 'impossible' situation because the treatment had got stuck and there seemed to be no way out of the impasse. In such situations, if they are serious enough, archetypal dreams are likely to occur which point out a possible line of advance one would never have thought of oneself. It is this kind of situation that

constellates the archetype with the greatest regularity. In certain cases the psychotherapist therefore sees himself obliged to discover the rationally insoluble problem towards which the patient's unconscious is steering. Once this is found, the deeper layers of the unconscious, the primordial images, are activated and the transformation of the personality can get underway.

With Jung's contextual depiction of the psychiatrist's role on the "world stage" fixed firmly in our minds, what is going on here should be clear enough.

Jung has before him in his office the perfect "modern" patient, ready, even *ripe* for his psychiatric "healing," for his religious, archetypal doctrine, for his professed "aim" of restoring the unbeliever to a "oneness" with the "God-image." His patient is *possessed* (S, 439) by the enemy, by the very demon of modernistic thought: she is *rationalistic*; she is steeped in a "Cartesian philosophy" to which she "rigidly clings." She has a strong scientific, or realistic, "outlook." Jung's job is to *shake her free* of that outlook, to break down her rationalism, her Cartesian habit of mind, to move her affectively toward the "religious outlook" that *all* his patients "over thirty-five" *require*. In a word, it is Jung's job *to save the woman's soul*. Not only does the "soul," for Jung, "correspond to God" (IRPPA, 10), but "psychology" is explicitly "the science of the soul" (IRPPA, 14) and the psychiatrist "one of those who know most about the conditions of the soul's welfare" (CT, 304). When we glance once again at Jung's letter to Freud (Feb. 11, 1910) in which Jung claims that "religion" (what his patient *lacks*) "can be replaced only by religion," we realize that Jung's consulting room functions as a *tabernacle*, as a place for the enactment of spiritual transformations, spiritual *conversions*. We do not know, of course, *exactly* what happens in Jung's office during the episode with the beetle, but we do know this: when the creature appears at the window Jung *seizes* upon an opportunity to *astonish* his patient and, *through* her astonishment, *to get the transference going*, for it is by means of *the transference* that Jung will be able to bring his patient over to *his* way of thinking. Jung does *not* say when the beetle appears, oh, what a striking coincidence, your dream and this rose-chafer. On the contrary, he says and does *something* to further his priestly purpose. He says and does *something* "dramatic and mythological" as he enacts his salvational role on the "world stage." Obviously, he succeeds. His patient is unable to withstand his oracular performance. Her *resistance* to the transference melts away, and she undergoes a "rebirth," a "process of transformation"–in short, *a relinquishment of her rational mind-set*. When Jung writes (S, 440) that a therapeutic crisis or "impasse" is most "likely" to lead to a "constellation of the archetype," and further, that it is the *therapist himself* who is sometimes "obliged to discover" the direction in which the patient's "unconscious" is "steering," he gives the whole tendentious business away unmistakably. It is *Jung* who is orchestrating the course of events in his consulting room. It is *Jung* who is "steering" his patient toward the archetypal realm, toward the world of unconscious, primitive images through which she may discover the *imago Dei* and the "transformation of the personality" she supposedly requires. Once she submits to the transference relationship, once she creates *a bond of dependency*, Jung's patient hasn't a chance. She is in a consulting room *designed* for religious conversions with a *convinced religionist* as a "psychotherapist." Jung can *use* the entrance of the beetle to establish the presence of God, or some such supernatural influence. He can *make* of a remarkable coincidence a witness to the existence of a higher power. He can "rejuvenate the dead sun-god" in accordance with the Egyptian Book of the *Netherworld*–the world of his patient's *unconscious*. (In psychoanalytic terms, Jung fosters an electrifying, "projection-making" moment during the course of which his shocked, startled patient can project her internalized object out into the environment where it may serve as a supernatural substitute for the relinquished parent.) Thus does Jung accomplish his cherished psychiatric *aim*. The putative archetypal, synchronistic event becomes a "sign," a sort of "miracle" against which this woman's *reason* is unable to hold firm. Instead of tracing his patient's symptoms back to their origins in infancy and childhood, instead of allowing his patient to better understand herself in a realistic psychological manner, Jung simply offers her his religion, his homemade magical pill as it were. After all, that's what she *needs*, is it not? Jung knows. He knows best. He knows that everyone requires a "religious outlook." Had Jung bothered to *observe* infants and children, had he *looked at* the early period, had he *studied* the initial stages of human development, he might have *seen* the way in which religion *inherits* the problems and the difficulties of our foundational years, and he might have helped his withdrawn, blocked patient to concentrate upon and work through precisely those problems and difficulties. The resulting insight might well have led to a *reasonable* "transformation," that is, to a fresh understanding of the self which would *not* be obliged to sacrifice a rationalistic mind-set. There was no *necessity* here for a regression to magical thinking. There was no *necessity* here for the "archetypal" upheaval Jung intentionally, controllingly orchestrates through his "psychiatric" manipulations. The beetle incident is often presented by Jungians (see Bolen 1982, 15) as a wonderful, "numinous" moment in Jung's wonderful, transformational writings, a moment in which we behold the salvation of a lost individual. To my mind, it is a sorry, even twisted moment, a kind of spiritual or intellectual rape, precipitated by the rigidity of Jung's "religious outlook," his insistence that people "get better" when they come over to *his* way of thinking. In the last analysis, Jung is the pastor's son all dressed up in self-styled oracular robes.

TRANSFERENTIAL SYNCHRONICITY

What happens in Jung's consulting room appears to be, with some variation of course, an integral aspect of Jungian theory and practice–particularly with regard to the role of the *transference* in the analyst-patient relationship. In C. A. Meier's (1986, 54) view, we should regard the *transference itself* as "an acausal relationship, in accordance with Jung's principle of synchronicity." During the midst of the transference, Meier (56) observes, "synchronistic events are experienced with some frequency." Why? "Practically every analyst becomes a savior-god to his patient, and this constellates an archetype which brings the [patient] powerful affluxes of emotion" (58). In such an intense transferential climate synchronicities are bound to occur, synchronicities which harbor the potential to "move" the patient out of his "stagnant" condition (59). Meier (188) concludes by suggesting that it is the "healer's task" to bring his patient to the archetypal level *"as a synchronistic event"* (my emphasis). For Bolen (1982, 33), "a deep connection must occur . . . for the analytic process to be effective," and when such a "connection" does in fact obtain, "synchronistic events" may take place. Indeed, claims Bolen (35), a powerful "transference" from patient to doctor "can lead to parapsychological phenomena," to "telepathic" messages and "extrasensory perceptions" from which "archetypal materials," including "synchronicity," emerge. It is the "interwoven shared psyche" of the "therapist and patient" that calls forth the "collective unconscious" (35-6). According to Robert Aziz (1990, 169), it is the "bonding" between "analyst" and "analysand" that explains a wide range of "synchronistic phenomena." Such "bonding" transpires beyond the "dimensions" of ordinary "time and space" (172); it removes the participants to a transcendent, "religious" realm best described in the literature of "shaminism" and "theological metaphysics" (174). As doctor and patient interact in this spiritual locale "synchronistic experiences . . . seem to increase . . . in proportion to the degree of unconscious identification between analyst and analysand" (174). J. Marvin Spiegelman (1996, 204), perhaps the leading Jungian analyst of the 1990's, sums things up very nicely for us in his volume,

Psychotherapy as a Mutual Process. Although the analyst and analysand "surely have a separate existence," at a "deeper level *they are both expressions of the same objective psyche*" (my emphasis). In fact, they are both involved in an "interdependency," in a "participation mystique," in an "ontic field" where their mutual communications pass transferentially from one unconscious mind to the other. Spiegelman describes this "deep mutual process" as "acausal"–the word Jung employs of course to indicate the nature of synchronistic occurrences. Spiegelman (198) strives to clarify matters for us by turning to atomic physics, to "quantum field-like phenomena" in which apparently separate items are linked inextricably together. He even produces a complex drawing, or diagram, in which psyches and archetypes graphically intertwine amidst a wealth of lines and arrows.

We may not know exactly what occurred in Jung's consulting room, but we do know, now, what is *designed* to occur in the offices of his loyal followers. The disclosures shed further, valuable light on the psychoanalytic nature and meaning of synchronicity. The relationship of analyst and analysand is rooted in the *transference*, in the regressive, affective bonding that restores the early period of our lives. This is the period in which the *parent* is the "savior-god" (Meier 1986, 54) of the *child*, in which the caregiver and the offspring "are both expressions of the same objective psyche" (Spiegelman 1966, 204), in which the existence of the maternal figure is "interwoven" (Bolen 1982, 35) with the existence of her charge. The "powerful affluxes of emotion" (Meier 1986, 58) that emerge during the course of the transference do not stem from some "archetype;" they stem from the transferential reawakening of the first relationship, the reawakening of the powerful emotional exchanges that transpired as the real child interacted intensely and sometimes imperfectly, with the real parent upon whom he depended and for whom he harbored a wide variety of feelings–from love and gratitude to hate and disappointment. The transference restores what is conceivably the most purely and potently affective stage of our lives. Having created a deep, transferential bond, having reactivated the early time in all its intimate, affective significance, analyst and patient begin to experience synchronicities *because synchronicities are a cardinal feature of the first relationship*, a cardinal expression, a cardinal manifestation, of the *affective attunement* in which the first relationship is *grounded*. We have already established this in considerable detail but we may call up the essentials again very briefly here. Often the caregiver knows the child's needs *before* the child announces them, "telepathically" or "clairvoyantly" as it were (Bolen 1982, 35). Frequently the caregiver arrives to assist the child *just as* the child requires her to do so, *synchronistically* as it were. Affective attunement *means*, in large measure, the good object's *good timing*. Conversely, the child may know the caregiver's mood before the caregiver overtly expresses her mood. The child may move the caregiver to act simply by willfully indicating his wishes. The child is deeply, unconsciously convinced of the caregiver's total devotion to his welfare. All the "paranormal, clairvoyant, telepathic" events that occur within the transference (Bolen 1982, 3) merely attest to the transference's tendency to restore the early period in which such events occur *over and over again*, on a *daily* basis. Synchronicities "increase" as the "unconscious identification between analyst and analysand" deepens (Aziz 1990, 169) because the deepening of the unconscious bond increases the intensity of the regression to the early time. More and more *attunement* between analyst and patient leads to more and more synchronicity. No wonder Meier (1986, 54) calls the *transference itself* "an acausal relationship, in accordance with Jung's principle of synchronicity." When Bolen (1982, 34) describes the analyst-patient bond as a mutual "unconscious mirroring" within a mutual "light trance state" she describes in what could be clinical psychoanalytic terms the very essence of the attuned parent-child interaction. We don't have to puzzle any longer about the psychological origin and meaning of synchronicity: it is the unconscious mnemic trace of our first relationship with the caregiver, an echo of the period in which the big one, the "macrocosm," watches over and addresses the needs of the little one, or "microcosm," in a clairvoyant, telepathic, synchronistic, *timely* fashion.

Now, here is the ultimate trick of the business. The synchronicities that are mutually sensed and shared in the Jungian consulting room during the course of the mirroring transference relationship are taken by analyst and patient (with the analyst leading the way, of course) to be a witness to the existence of the archetypal realm, the collective unconscious, the all-embracing Tao in which everything is connected to everything else through a pre-established harmony or *attunement*. What in reality constitutes proof of regression to the early period is *employed* as support for the existence of Jung's spiritual universe. And what *follows* is more or less inevitable, that is, if the "treatment" works, and if the analyst is willing to let his client *go*. As the patient comes to believe, through synchronicity, that he has touched the archetypal level, touched the collective unconscious, touched the all-embracing Tao, he comes to feel himself more and more connected, integrated, attached, secure, more and more *at one* with the world. He is no longer "alienated," no longer alone, isolated, cut off–and he is also, increasingly, *no longer in need of the analyst* whose job it is to shift the patient's regressive tie to *himself* onto the Jungian "archetypes," the *imago Dei*, the "God within," the "individuated self," the *imago Dei*, the "God within," the "individuated self," represented by the mandala. Remember, the patient is *already regressed*, already in the midst of the re-created early time; he is already experiencing the "powerful affluxes of emotion" that he originally experienced in relation to the caregiver. Thus he is ready to be joined with a substitute object; indeed, he has *already* been joined with a substitute in the shape of the *analyst*. Can anyone fail to realize, at precisely this juncture, that an *archetype* is an *internalized object*? As normal development transpires, the child shifts his original attachment to the caregiver onto the caregiver's transitional, illusory substitutes (Winnicott). He turns creatively to the symbolical realm, and he eventually puts "God" in the parent's place as his protector and provider. In the Jungian consulting room, the patient moves psychologically from the caregiver in the person of the analyst, or better, from the caregiver as she is *restored* in the person of the analyst, to what the analyst is offering as a substitute for the original object, namely the archetypal realm whose existence is established through the very synchronicities that in reality restore the early period of affective attunement. This virtually impenetrable Jungian scheme provides the emotionally needy patient with a chance to *do all over again* what most of us do once and for all during the early years as we choose our original and permanent substitutes for the lost or relinquished parent. In this way, Jungian analysis *is* the early period *the second time around*. Those who seek it out are "having problems" in the "modern world," just as Jung says. They cannot find through the customary religions the attachment and the succoring they require; their original illusions (Winnicott) *don't work*. They are "uprooted wraiths" who have been torn from the "womb" of "tradition." In the Jungian consulting room, however, these spiritual seekers find a *new* religion, a new transcendent realm of symbols to which they may attach themselves and through which they may terminate their uprootedness. They find the world of the archetype, the world of the collective unconscious, the world of the all-embracing Tao, the world Jung has *provided* for them through his spiritual creations, for as Jung declares, "religion can be replaced only by religion" (letter to Freud, Feb. 11, 1910). Nor do they doubt or misgive (assuming they are able to enter into the transference): they have witnessed the existence of the archetypal realm through the remarkable synchronicities that have passed between themselves and the Jungian analyst. In a figurative sense, they have *seen the beetle*.

MIRACLES OF GRACE, ABSOLUTELY

As a pathway to Jung's new religious universe, as a witness to the immediacy, to the proximity, of the divine, as an incontrovertible proof of the world's loving, caring, nurturing nature, synchronicity gets bathed in the Jungian literature with lush religious language and with time-honored religious conceptualization. When the dust settles, when the pseudo-scientific smokescreen of quantum mechanics, and probability, and holography disappears, synchronicity emerges for exactly what it is: a wish-fulfilling, religious illusion, a simple, regressive, unconscious insistence that something is out there watching over us, a simple, regressive, unconscious denial that separation from the caregiver is an accomplished fact. Synchronicity is religiously clear to the hearts of its adherents because it says to them, you're not your own after all. Let's listen to some of the language; let's sample a few of the conceptualizations.

When we realize through the witnessing of "synchronistic events," writes Jung (A, 260-61), that "the psyche cannot be totally different from matter," we are "initiated into the mysteries," into the "mystic transformation process," just as the ancients at Eleusis and the early Christians in the Holy Land were initiated. As we engage the "synchronistic" realm we are "restored, rejuvenated, changed;" we are ushered into "transcendent territory," into the world of the "miraculous." Indeed, declares Jung, "synchronicity" makes it plain that "miracles " are "possible" (S, 530), that "prayer" is "efficacious," (S, 518), that we participate as human beings in the "continuous creation of a pattern that exists from all eternity" (S, 518). One is tempted to breathe, amen. With Jung's beetle in the forefront of his mind, Scott Peck (1988, 259-60) sets out to demonstrate for us synchronicity's divine significance: he is struggling at his writing desk with a particularly difficult passage when his wife walks in unexpectedly and hands him just the volume he needs to resolve his dilemma. Peck writes, "this was not a stupendous event. There were no trumpets to announce it ... Nevertheless, *I was touched by grace*" (my emphasis). It was as if Jung's "beetle" had "tapped" on *his* "windowpane." Although synchronistic events happen to him "all the time," Peck (259) confesses, he is not always fully aware of "their *miraculous nature*" (my emphasis), of their ability to "nurture" his "spiritual growth" (260). Incidentally, when Peck (260) observes that synchronicities occur "frequently," that "their action is either incompletely understandable ... or totally obscure," and that they cannot be "influenced by human consciousness" or "the process of conscious decision-making," he merely underscores what we have been maintaining all along in this book. Synchronicity occurs "frequently" because we are frequently reminded of the early period when the caregiver was out there watching over us; synchronicity is "incompletely understandable" or "obscure" because we cannot see directly into our unconscious associations and motivations; synchronicity cannot be "influenced by human consciousness" or "conscious decision-making" because we cannot control the return of the repressed, our tendency to *project* our wishes into the environment. What Peck presents as otherworldly and mysterious is perfectly naturalistic and straightforward from a psychoanalytic angle.

According to Victor Mansfield (1995, 6-7), "synchronistic experiences" provide us with a "glimpse" into the "higher reality." They appear as "epiphanies" or "bestowals of grace." Most of all, however, they enable us to correct one of our most persistent mental errors, namely our "belief in our separateness and independence." Synchronicities, claims Mansfield, destroy this "troubling view of ourselves," this "despiritualized" outlook that so many of us carry around. For precisely this reason, synchronicities take us in the direction of "healing." Synchronicity, says Progoff (1973, 104-05), is rooted in "the archetype of hope," the hope that "the miracle will happen." Yet this archetype itself, Progoff informs us as he recalls a personal conversation with Jung should actually be thought of as "the archetype of the miracle," or "the archetype of magical effect." This is because synchronicities are "uncanny" or "transfixing" occurrences which take us directly to the realm of "numinosity," a "primal" level of the mind where "the process of differentiation into the opposites of life has not yet been carried through" (111). Here we find "the aura of great light," the aura of "great warmth" (108). Could there be a more striking, disguised expression of the wish for symbiotic fusion with the object? Synchronicity, for Bolen (1982, 9), attests to the "greater whole," to the "stillness of God" at the "heart of all activity." It tells us, in Robert Browning's famous words, that "God is in heaven," and "all is right with the world" (23). Is not this but another way of stating, asks Bolen, that the "Holy Spirit" surrounds us? Of course it is, for "what happens in our lives apparently by chance or fortune is not really accidental" (61); it is directed by the "Synchronistic Matchmaker," the divinity that brings the miraculous into our lives, the divinity that weds us to the eternal. Evoking "spiritual reality," the "synchronistic moment," Bolen concludes (103), links us to the "cosmic matrix," terminates our "separation" and "loneliness," provides us with a "numinous, religious . . . sense of oneness." And so it goes in Bolen, on and on and on, in the same wish-fulfilling vein. Writes the famous Jungian scholar, Erich Neumann (1979, 117): "If the premise of synchronicity . . . can be validated this would mean . . . phenomena which have ... been described in theological terms as 'miracles' are in principle contained in the structure of our world." Finally, in the view of Sidney Handel (1993, 387), when synchronicity occurs it validates the notion of the "miraculous" in our lives. Accordingly, maintains Handel, the "proto-type" of synchronicity in general should be "the people of Israel at the Red Sea." Handel dubs his discussion, *Mirabili Dictu*, a title that has, to my ear at least, the ring of Vatican City and the official publications of the Church.

It can hardly come as a surprise to the reader in this lush spiritual context of miracles and divine grace that Jungian synchronicities awaken in those who experience them feelings of religious conviction, religious certainty–absolute and indisputable *religious knowledge*. After all, when one watches the Red Sea part one is apt to be impressed by the event. "Synchronistic phenomena," writes Jung (S, 506), are accompanied by a feeling of "absolute knowledge." Grounded in the archetype, they have nothing to do with the intellect, with reason, with philosophical niceties or proofs. They have to do, rather, with the "belly," with affect, with a meaning that is both "self-subsistent" and "subjectively convincing." Robert Aziz (1990, 77-8) is in full agreement: "in that synchronistic experiences arise out of an archetypal ground, they have associated with them ... a numinous or spiritual charge that announces itself to the subject primarily on the feeling level." What "counts" here is not "philosophical argument" but "religious conviction," the degree to which the subject is "gripped" by the moment. Aziz draws things together as follows (78):

> with synchronistic experiences of 'absolute knowledge' the affect-laden numinous charge is usually experienced first when the archetypal content enters consciousness, and second when the corresponding external event is observed [translation: the return of the repressed triggers a wish-fulfilling projection].

Write Combs and Holland (1990, 73-79), "for the individual caught up by the power of the archetype, the symbolic meaning of his or her life is no abstraction but a powerfully felt and utterly convincing reality." And then, specifically with reference to our topic, synchronicity "carries with it the feeling of numinosity or absolute cosmic authority." When we actually "live" a "synchronicity," we experience it at the "deep ... dramaturgical level," the level of the unconscious mind where Jung's affective, arche-typal approach "stands the test of time." Similar views may be found in Jacobi (1959, 66) and von Franz (1980, 39).

Here we must simply back off. I mean, there is no *arguing*, no *reasoning* with all this. We are in the midst of *religion*–the numinous, the miraculous, the divine, the kind of "absolute knowledge" we associate with those who have been "spiritually changed" or "spiritually reborn." We've all confronted our fellow human beings in the midst of such *enthusiasm*, such *fanaticism*, of course; we've all seen the passionate, inflexible, not-to-be-reasoned with look in their eyes. We've all heard their exclamations, their intimate, heartfelt claims: "I experienced this synchronicity for myself, man; God is *out there*; I *know* it, in my *guts*." The point is, this is *exactly* where synchronicity *belongs*; this is *exactly* where synchronicity ultimately *resides–not* in the realm of physics or probability or holography, but in the realm of *religion*, the realm of *absolute knowledge, of spiritual certainty*, of the fervent, fanatical *wish* for a supernatural connection to the world. Once the unconscious has provided the individual with a projective re-attachment to the caregiver, once the torment of separation and aloneness has been erased by the wish-fulfilling illusion of attachment, *nothing is going to take it away*. The individual hangs on to his soothing belief like a bulldog. Indeed, the *absoluteness* of his newly found "knowledge" is the affective witness to the intensity of the discomfort that resides in separation, in being on one's own in the vast universe. The *crises* of the early period, along with their later derivatives, are resolved by the synchronistic proof of the caregiver's abiding, otherworldly presence.

This is why synchronicity is associated routinely with *crisis*, why a synchronistic incident is likely to transpire when an individual discovers himself in an emotional dilemma or at an emotional impasse, why Handel's (1993, 387) figure of the "children of Israel at the Red Sea," or the children of Israel *in crisis*, is a suitable backdrop for the occurrence of synchronistic events. Note these further brief substantiations from the Jungian literature. Archetypal experiences including synchronicity, states Jung (S, 457), "generally appear in times of psychic disorientation in order to compensate a chaotic state." And again, "insecure conditions" draw forth "magical" effects "in the most natural way" (SDP, 45). We might think here again on the transformational beetle Jung shows to his patient in the midst of her emotional "impasse," her crisis of "rigidity" (S, 439). Synchronistic happenings, writes Aziz (1990, 65), reach into an individual's "heart of hearts" with the power to heal "the sense of grief" which typically accompanies the death of a loved one, the crisis of *loss*. Observe Combs and Holland (1990, 85): "periods of major life transitions" seem to be accompanied "by an abundance of meaningful coincidence ... The period of mid-life transition, or *mid-life crisis*, is visited by more than its share of synchronicity." And then, "the most dramatic transition of all is death . . . No other event . . . is associated with so rich an array of psychic phenomena." Crises of "isolation," maintains Bolen (1982, 22-3), often "result" in "synchronistic events," events which enable the "isolated" individual to feel both "an affinity to others" and a "connection to the divine." It is during "periods of inner insecurity" or within "states of disorientation" that "synchronicities" are apt to occur.

Crisis pushes open the door to synchronicity because the individual *in crisis* seeks assistance, seeks a helpmate as it were, a someone or a something that can resolve the dilemma, terminate the impasse, lessen the stress. As a regression to the *idealized past*, as a link to the original helpmate, the original "savior-god," synchronicity is a "natural" projective strategy for coping with the *anxiety-laden present*. To express the matter from another, related angle, synchronicity is apt to occur in crisis (isolation, insecurity, grief, loss, death) because crisis is apt to reach *all the way down* to our primal levels of anxiety, the anxiety that is unconsciously associated with our *first* crisis, our first "fall from paradise," our first, primal disruption and loss, namely our separation from the caregiver, our separation from the "savior-god" of our infancy and childhood. The synchronistic event is unconsciously designed to *restore* that "numinous" presence to our distraught, precarious lives; it is designed to reassure us and thus to assist us in the "hour of our need." Crisis is the soil in which *all* the wish-fulfilling illusions of religion tend to flourish, and synchronicity is ultimately but another wish-fulfilling, religious illusion. Had Jung looked at the initial stages of human existence, had he paid some professional attention to the early period, had he observed infants and children coping with separation by turning to illusory, substitute objects, he might have spied the projective, symptomatic connection between crisis and the synchronistic event. Jung's theory of synchronicity must bear the weight of this glaring omission.

FROM MATER TO MATTER AND BACK AGAIN: THE SYNCHRONICITY OF SYNCHRONICITY

For Jung and his followers, modern man is in search of a soul. He is spiritually barren, spiritually bankrupt, adrift is a disgodded, fragmented world. Modern man's spiritual plight is rooted in the Age of Reason (ca 1620-1780), the Enlightenment, the rise of science and technology, a cultural, historical development which has led, on the one hand, to the decline of traditional religion (Nietzsche's "God is dead"), and on the other, to a view of nature as lifeless and exploitable. To look upon nature as lifeless and exploitable, as *mere dead matter* to be *used*, is to *relinquish*

the age-old view of nature as a nurturing, creative, containing entity–
Mater, Mother Nature, the womb of life and the world. "Between the
sixteenth and seventeenth centuries," writes Carolyn Merchant (1980, xvi),
"the image of an organic cosmos with a living female earth at its center
gave way to a mechanistic world view in which nature was reconstructed
as dead and passive, to be dominated and controlled by humans." By the
nineteenth century, the century of Jung's youth and early development, the
"dead world" of "Newtonian mechanics" and the "urban world" of economics and trade were flourishing very vigorously throughout Europe and
America (276). "Living animate nature died, while dead inanimate money
was endowed with life" (288). Merchant concludes, "increasingly capital
and the market would assume the organic attributes of growth, strength,
activity, pregnancy, weakness, decay, and collapse, obscuring and mysti-
fying the new underlying social relations of production and reproduction
that make economic growth and progress possible . . . Perhaps the ultimate
irony in these transformations was the new name given them: rationality"
(288). Here is Brian Easlea (1981, 70-3) on the same topic and quoting the
seventeenth-century thinkers who stood behind the new, scientific spirit:
"the experimental philosophy was, as Oldenburg had explicitly stated it to
be, a masculine philosophy, and its goal was to be the properly masculine
one . . . of knowing–to quote Glanvill–'the ways of *captivating* Nature,
and making her *subserve* our purposes, thereby achieving the Empire of
Man over Nature.'" Easlea goes on, "Descartes, in common with all
mechanical philosophers, believed that he could explain all natural phenomena in terms of . . . particles of matter" (72-3). Thus, "devoid of mind
and thought, devoid of sentience, devoid of occult forces, of sympathies
and antipathies, . . . nature had been transformed in the minds of the
mechanical philosophers from a semi-divine, creative maternal figure to
mere . . . matter and motion" (73). What the "mechanical philosophy
amounted to was . . . a radical 'de-mothering' of nature and the earth in
preparation for, and in legitimation of, the technological appropriation of
the natural world that the mechanical philosophers hoped they and their
successors would undertake" (73). Two-hundred years after "the initial
formulation of the mechanical philosophy," concludes Easlea (73), its
precepts were firmly established throughout most of Western culture. To
properly understand Jung's new religious psychology we must view it in
the light of these major historical events.

"Things have gone rapidly downhill since the Age of Enlightenment,"
writes Jung (IRPPA, 16), who regards the rise of "science and technology"
as "Luciferian" (A, 36), that's right, *Luciferian*, of the *devil*. To rectify the
situation, Jung creates his archetypal psychology, a psychology designed

to restore "man" to "nature," not nature as *matter*, as lifeless and exploit-able, the Enlightenment view, but nature as *Mater*, alive, organic, succor-ing, enveloping. "Whether he understands them or not," Jung declares (ACV, 93), "man must remain conscious of the world of the archetypes, because in it he is still a part of Nature and is connected with his own roots. A view of the world or a social order that cuts him off from the primordial images of life not only is no culture at all but, in increasing degree, is a prison or a stable." Jung goes on, "[man] knows that the mother carries for us that inborn image of the *mater natura* and *mater spiritualis*, of the totality of life of which we are a small and helpless part." Indeed, "our mother," our "accidental carrier," ultimately represents "the whole of created nature," the "experience of life whose children we are." And then, in those poetical syllables at which we glanced earlier, "the mother is the first world of the child and the last world of the adult. We are all wrapped as her children in the mantle of this great Isis" (ACU, 94). In this way, to be a "modern man" is, for Jung (CT, 75), to be "estranged" from oneself, to be "unhistorical in the deepest sense," torn from the "maternal womb" of "tradition" in which the "mass of men" has always resided. It will be helpful here to recall Jung's lifelong interest in and devotion to *matriarchy*, his belief that, at the social level, "a return to the mother" would be beneficial or "revitalizing," and his belief that, at the individual level, "we are reborn . . . through a return to the realm of the mothers" (Noll 1994, 173-4). We might also recall at this juncture Jung's *consulting room*, his attempt to guide his "Cartesian" (S, 439) patient toward *rebirth* by breaking down her scientific spirit, the "rationalism" which, as Jung puts it, "possesses" her (Lucifer?). For Jung, the *beetle* is an instrument of the "irrational" (S, 439), the imaginal, the archetypal, the instinctual, a means of terminating the *rule of reason*. Accordingly, the beetle appears to be a guide to the *mother's domain*. We need not rely entirely, however, on these pronounced, objectified witnesses to Jung's mother-centered aims and beliefs. To achieve the understanding we seek, we have only to remind ourselves of the manner in which Jung projec-tively and metaphorically ascribes to the religious, archetypal universe into which he would lead us the cardinal features of the *first relationship between the mother and the infant*: it is a universe of "pre-established harmony," of "one common breathing," of "one common flow," a universe in which each separate substance, each *blind monad*, "mirrors" or "re-flects" all the others, "binding" and "knitting" them together as parts of a single, "living organism" (S, 490-99). If the Enlightenment, as Easlea (1981, 73) says, accomplished the "de-mothering" of the world, then Jung's archetypal psychology is designed in significant measure to "re-mother" it.

Note how Jung's followers bear the matter out. According to Feinstein and Krippner's *Personal Mythology* (1988, 216), "the conquering hero of the contemporary era has ripped himself away from Mother Nature, spearheaded by a belligerent personal ego and supported by increasingly sophisticated technology." Things have gone entirely "too far" and "with this," the "great revaluation of the feminine begins." We have "repressed the Great Mother," say these authors, a "disastrous" occurrence, and our present spiritual job is to end our "alienation" by "welcoming" her into our lives again (216-17). For Combs and Holland (1990, xx-xxix), "the myth of the mechanistic universe" has prompted us to forget or deny "the soul;" we have been "robbed" of our "sense of wonder." As an antidote, we must once again take up Kepler's idea that "the earth itself [is] animated by an inherent spiritual nature." Better still, we can turn to the work of James Lovelock in which nature appears as "Gaia," the "earth goddess" of antiquity. This would lead us back to the time-honored notion of "earth" as a "living organism." In the view of C.A. Meier (1986, 303), "man is estranged from his soul, therefore from his own inner nature, by being lost in the outer world." He is "cut off" from nature, "alienated" from nature, and his "soul" suffers accordingly: "as the natural sciences developed, respect for Nature as a whole disappeared. We no longer bring sacrifices to her, we think of having dominated her, and to a large extent we *have* dominated her to a point where the original fear of Nature has disappeared. What does inner nature (microcosm) say to that loss of fear?" asks Meier. "We find that we have lost something equilibriating, equalizing, sane, and valuable." Unless we return to "Nature" and stop "wounding" her, we are in "great danger," for "Nature" is where "the archetypes live" (311). Nature is "the unconscious, the earth, our mother, Mother Nature" (311). Writes Jungian historian Richard Tarnas (1993, 44): "the crisis of modern man is essentially masculine crisis," and the "deepest passion of the Western mind has been to reunite with the ground of its own being" (443). This means, according to Tarnas, the "reintegration of the repressed feminine," and a "sacrifice" of the "masculine ego." Only through "the embrace of the feminine" will alienated Western man find the means to fulfill his inner being and to achieve a "new reality" (444-45). Tarnas titles the chapter in which he promulgates these opinions, "Bringing It All Back Home."

This turn to the "feminine," this gravitation toward a mother-centered, matriarchal outlook, does not restrict itself, of course, to the new religious psychology of Jung and his followers; on the contrary, it is a central feature of the new spirituality, including the New Age, and in some

measure an angry, passionate reaction to what is regarded by large numbers of people as an inextricable link between patriarchal theology and
materialistic pursuit. The whole business is summed up nicely in an issue
of *Maclean's Magazine* (April 8, 1996) devoted to the question, Is God a
Woman? Writes Marci McDonald (50):

> as that debate continues to rage on, a few optimists believe that, in fact,
> a new concept of divinity is trying to manifest itself in the world.
> 'There's something trying to be born that has elements of Mother Earth
> and transcendence,' says Ron Graham. 'People are searching for a new
> articulation of the eternal questions. And I think that new articulation
> will have more of a feminine quality.' But, he cautions, 'it's going to
> take hundreds of years to go through.'

McDonald's fine, readable article is loaded with information on "the
booming goddess revival" among neo-pagans, on the new hymnal of the
United Church with its praises directed toward "God, the All-Holy, Maker
and Mother," on the spate of recent books dealing with "women's spirituality," and on the new "spiritual tourism" featuring trips to the matriarchal
shrines of the ancient world. We may be moving "beyond God the Father,"
states McDonald; we may be replacing the traditional occupant of "the
house of God." Let's bring all this together now from a psychoanalytic
angle.

    With the Enlightenment and its aftermath, including the death of God
and the death of Nature (*mater* into matter), increasing numbers of people
can no longer escape the primal anxiety of separation from the caregiver
through the traditional illusions of Western spirituality. The creative,
transitional realm of symbolical substitution undergoes a major upheaval
which involves for many not only the loss of the centerpiece, God the
Father, but the loss of the creative, illusory realm *itself*. To express the
matter informally, there is "no place" for *the crisis*, the *original* crisis, the
crisis of the *early period*, "to go." There is no way to drain off the anxiety
that accrues as a separation from the maternal figure leads developmentally to a full-fledged sense of individuality, autonomy, egotic selfhood,
differentiation from the environment and from other people. *The crisis of
the early period becomes interwoven with the crisis of the social world.*
Moreover, the crises that occur *after* the early period closes, the crises that
inherit the *primal* anxieties, the crises that reach all the way down to the
original loss, the original expulsion from the Garden (I am thinking of
injury, illness, death, divorce), are left *hanging* for want of spiritual
support, spiritual refuge, spiritual comfort. The "modern" preoccupation
with "the abyss," with meaninglessness, lack of purpose, alienation and the

rest, is in many instances but a symptomatic *acting-out* of the emotional, affective emptiness that results from the loss of the original caregiver. What is psychological and primary is elevated to the secondary level, the level of philosophical and theological discussion. Life becomes potentially *meaningless* because there is nothing *in life* to replace the first engenderer of meaning, or better, the first engenderer of the *loving attachment* which is *meaning's ground*. For many others, needless to say, the death of God and Nature merely leads to *new gods*, to new creative, illusory substitutions for the maternal object. Some turn to ideology or money or interpersonal relationships as they seek to fulfill their search for meaning, for purpose, for attachment and security; others turn to reason, or to science. As Jung observes, "you can take away a man's gods, but only to give him others in return" (CT, 280). Among these "others" is *mater* in various shapes and forms, as the "goddess," as Isis, as the *matriarch* of "feminine spirituality" whose fortunes begin to rise in earnest at about the time Nietzsche and Jung arrive on the scene. The feminine, matriarchal leaning has been there all along, of course; it is as old as civilization. But it gets a major boost, a major goad as it were, from the Enlightenment and its aftermath. As God the Father fades into Deism, as He becomes a kind of Newtonian designer of physical laws, the old, affective thirst for the mother (never far from the surface) awakens vigorously. With the Father-God no longer absorbing the early anxieties over separation and loss--the fundamental, internalized *angst* that attends differentiation and the onset of autonomy--such anxieties find their way quite smoothly and naturally to the Mother-God who is, after all, *closer* to the original, affective issue than is the patriarchal deity. Indeed, it may very well be that, with the death of God, the unconscious spies an *opportunity* to bring the mother in, to replace the father with the primary object of desire. The Enlightenment may *legitimate* the search for the parent with the breasts by dethroning or discrediting the parent with the penis. Now, Jung's theory of synchronicity must be seen as an integral part of this cultural upheaval, an integral part of this cultural dilemma or crisis. I mean, it is hardly a *coincidence* that just as God and Nature are dying, just as science and reason and *materialism* are lowering God and Nature into their graves, Jung comes forward with a theory of *coincidence* that projects the original object out into the world as caregiver and reanimates the universe or Nature with a watchful spiritual presence, a something or a someone to which our lives are *meaningfully attached* (matter into *mater*). We may think of this as *the synchronicity of synchronicity*. Jung's theory emerges 1) just as it is needed to slake the bitter thirst for connection and meaning and 2) as part of the growing trend to replace God-the-Father with God-the-Mother.

Through synchronicity, through precisely Jung's theory of *meaningful coincidence*, the "modern" subject, the lost, goddess, "uprooted wraith," is provided with an opportunity to rediscover the maternal figure in the world, to rediscover a someone or a something that is watching, witnessing, assisting, *making miracles*. Jung even tries to give his theory scientific support, nay *justification*–to bring science over to religion's side along with psychoanalysis. For the "modern" subject is, truth told, a child of the Enlightenment; accordingly, he will be reassured that his unconscious wish for the caregiver is grounded in objective, scientific fact. That Jung's projective caregiver *is* unconsciously modeled on the mother we have already established in detail through our analysis of Jung's projective, metaphorical system, his reliance on Schopenhauer, Leibniz, Albertus Magnus, Hippocrates, and a number of other Western and Eastern sources.

For writers such as Colin Wilson (1984) and Arthur Koestler (1972), as we have seen, Jung's essay *On Synchronicity* is an obscure, meandering, scattered piece of work full of irrelevancies and dead ends. What, after all, have telepathy and clairvoyance and levitation and ESP *to do* with improbable coincidences? We cannot account fully for the peculiar nature of Jung's production. We cannot know with absolute assurance what was going through his mind as he put his pen to paper. Yet it may help us to remember that synchronicity as a concept and as an event removes one regressively to the world of infancy and childhood, to the particular perceptual nature, or phenomenology, of that period in our lives. Jung writes his essay with his *whole* mind, including his unconscious mind: there is no way for him, or for anyone, ever, to circumvent that. Accordingly, Jung deals with telepathy, and clairvoyance, and ESP, and the rest, in *On Synchronicity* because such items characterize perceptually the "amodal" mentation of the newcomer (Stern 1985) as he interacts with the world, including of course the caregiver, during the early stages of his existence. Jung's essay is a kind of gigantic *slip*, a gigantic *projection of the perceptual universe out of which synchronicity arises*. It has an obscure, disorganized quality or "feeling" because it reflects the unconscious side of Jung's interest in the subject. Jung fails to present us directly with the world of infancy and childhood in his work. But in *On Synchronicity* he gives us a glimpse of that world indirectly, inadvertently, purely as a witness to his own capacity for re-finding it at the dynamic level of his psychological speculations.

From precisely this angle we can also better understand the disruptive conflict between Jung and his early master, Freud. We know that Freud was disturbed by Jung's increasing reluctance to accept the foundational nature of sexuality in human behavior. Freud was also bothered by Jung's religious tendencies. We know, too, that Freud was concerned about Jung's gradual but persistent withdrawal from the role of loyal disciple, by Jung's urge to stand professionally on his own two feet. However, it may also be that Freud was profoundly threatened in his own unconscious mind by Jung's turn toward the mother's realm, by Jung's steady gravitation toward a mother-centered psychology, already in clear evidence by the time of the break (ca 1912-13). Although Freud was able to look closely and steadily at the oedipal period and at the father's place in the child's world, he was unwilling to look closely and steadily at the pre-oedipal phase and at the mother's role in the developmental picture. It was his own deep-seated anxiety that stood behind this facet of his character, and behind this facet of his theoretical bent. Conversely, we know that Jung was disturbed by the nature of Freud's sexual theories, by Freud's hostility toward the religious universe, and by Freud's authoritarian inclinations. Yet it might also be that Freud's oedipally-centered, father-centered, patriarchal psychology *impeded Jung's own unconscious gravitation toward the mother's realm*, his tendency to re-find and re-inhabit the pre-oedipal world of symbiotic attachment and blurred ego boundaries, the *world from which his theory of synchronicity ultimately derives*. Just as Freud was threatened by the direction of Jung's thought, so Jung was threatened by the direction of Freud's. The older man did not want to *go* where the younger man was taking him, that is, to the world of the mother, and the younger man did not want to be *held back* from that world. In this way, Jung's theory of synchronicity may well be a key not only to his psychological system, as the experts tell us (Aziz 1990), but to his own personal and professional history as well.

CHAPTER THREE'S LAST WORD

With the context of this book fixed firmly in our minds, we will not find it difficult to understand why synchronicity has become such a going concern, such an integral part of the current spiritual scene. How comforting it is, how reassuring it is, to go about believing the caregiver is out there, ministering to our needs. How natural it is to project the maternal figure into the environment, to hang on to the loving presence with whom we were so powerfully bonded and from whom we separated with such agony and sorrow as little ones. At the same time, for some of us at least, it is exciting and gratifying to set our illusions aside, to face reality straight on, to take a deep psychological breath, as it were, and confront life just as it is and not as we would wish it to be. Are not these two, fundamental tendencies–endlessly antithetical, endlessly combative, endlessly struggling one against the other–the very tendencies that define us as people, the very tendencies that mark us out as the human creature? We would go back, back to the mother, back to the source, the womb, and we would go forward into the unknown, the uncharted internal and external territories, the great fathomless universe that has opened before us and the great fathomless universe of the mind. There are, needless to say, adaptational, evolutional advantages to feeling attached and secure in the world, connected to the matrix, the root. A calm, relatively stress-free animal is likely to function better than an animal burdened with anxiety. Yet our evolutional bent is also, unquestionably, to *see*, to perceive things clearly, to drop the fantasies and myths that soothe us and lessen our stress as they cloud and distort our vision. I am no prophet, and I have no idea where the matter will end, if it ever ends. But I do know this: I would rather have one moment of honest, face-to-face perception of things as they are, no matter how much anxiety that engenders, than have a lifetime of comforting illusions.

NOTE

1. Here is the key to Chapter Three's references to the works of Jung (except for letters which are indicated by date):

A	Aion
ACU	Archetypes of the Collective Unconscious
AS	Alchemical Studies
CT	Civilization in Transition
IRPPA	Introduction to the Religious and Psychological Problems of Alchemy
NP	On the Nature of the Psyche
PR	Psychology and Religion: West and East
S	On Synchronicity: An Acausal Connecting Principle
SDP	The Structure and Dynamics of the Psyche
ST	Symbols of Transformation
TEAP	Two Essays on Analytical Psychology

REFERENCES

Aziz, R. 1990. *C.G. Jung's Psychology of Religion and Synchronicity.* Albany: State University of New York Press.

Bolen, J. 1982. *The Tao of Psychology: Synchronicity and the Self.* San Francisco: Harper and Row.

———. 1985. *Goddesses in Everywoman: A New Psychology of Women.* New York: Harper and Row.

————. 1990. *Gods in Everyman: A New Psychology of Men's Lives and Loves.*
New York: Harper and Row.

Bollas, C. 1987. *The Shadow of the Object: Psychoanalysis of the Unthought-Known.* London: Free Association Books.

Charet, F. 1993. *Spiritualism and the Foundation of C.G. Jung's Psychology.*
Albany: State University of New York Press.

Combs, A. and Holland, M. 1990. *Synchronicity: Science, Myth, and the Trickster.*
New York: Paragon House.

Easlea, B. 1981. *Science and Sexual Repression: Patriarchy's Confrontation with Women and Nature.* London: Weidenfeld and Nicolson.

Edinger, E. 1972. *Ego and Archetype: Individuation and the Religious Function of the Psyche.* New York: G.P. Putnam's Sons.

Feinstein, D., and Kripper, S. 1988. *Personal Mythology.* New York: Tarcher.

Handel, S. 1993. "Mirabile Dictu." *Proceedings of the Twelfth International Congress for Analytical Psychology,* ed. M. Mattoon. Einsiedeln, Switz.:
Daimon Verlag.

Jacobi, J. 1959. *Complex, Archetype, Symbol in the Psychology of C.G. Jung.*
Princeton: Princeton University Press.

Jung, C. 1967. *Alchemical Studies. Collected Works,* vol. 20. Princeton: Princeton University Press.

————. 1970. *Symbols of Transformation. Collected Works,* vol. 5. Princeton:
Princeton University Press.

————. 1970. *Two Essays on Analytical Psychology. Collected Works,* vol. 7.
Princeton: Princeton University Press.

————. 1973. *Letters,* vols. 1 and 2. Princeton: Princeton University Press.

————. 1974. *Introduction to the Religious and Psychological Problems of Alchemy. Collected Works,* vol. 12. Princeton: Princeton University Press.

————. 1975. *Aion. Collected Works,* vol. 9, part 2. Princeton: Princeton University Press.

————. 1975. *Civilization in Transition. Collected Works,* vol. 10. Princeton:
Princeton University Press.

————. 1981. *On Synchronicity: An Acuasal Connecting Principle.* In *The Structure and Dynamics of the Psyche. Collected Works,* vol. 8. Princeton:
Princeton University Press.

————. 1981. *On the Nature of the Psyche. Collected Works,* vol. 12. Princeton:
Princeton University Press.

————. 1981. *The Structure and Dynamics of the Psyche. Collected Works,* vol. 8.
Princeton: Princeton University Press.

————. 1982. *Psychology and Religion: West and East. Collected Works,* vol. 11.
Princeton: Princeton University Press.

————. 1990. *Archeytpes of the Collective Unconscious. Collected Works,* vol. 9,
Part 1. Princeton: Princeton University Press.

Koestler, A. 1972. *The Roots of Coincidence.* New York: Random House.

————. 1978. *Janus: A Summing Up.* New York: Random House.

McDonald, M. 1996. "Is God a Woman?" *Maclean's Magazine*, April 8, pp.46-51.

Malinowski, B. 1982. "Sorcery as Mimetic Representation." In *Witchcraft and Sorcery*, ed. M.Marwick. London: Penguin.

Mansfield, V. 1995. *Synchronicity, Science, and Soul-Making*. Chicago: Open Court.

Meier, C. 1986. *Soul and Body: Essays on the Theories of C.G. Jung*. San Francisco: Lapis Press.

Merchant, C. 1980. *The Death of Nature*. New York: Harper and Row.

Mitchell, S. 1988. *Relational Concepts in Psychoanalysis*. Cambridge, Mass.: Harvard University Press.

Neumann, E. 1979. *Creative Man*. Princeton: Princeton University Press.

Noll, R. 1994. *The Jung Cult: Origins of a Charismatic Movement*. Princeton: Princeton University Press.

Peat, F. 1987. *Synchronicity: The Bridge Between Matter and Mind*. New York: Bantam Books.

Peck, S. 1988. *The Road Less Traveled*. New York: Simon and Schuster.

Progoff, I. 1973. *Jung, Synchronicity and Human Destiny: C.G. Jung's Theory of Meaningful Coincidence*. New York: Julian Press.

Roheim, G. 1955. *The Origin and Function of Magic*. New York: International Universities Press.

Schafer, R. 1968. *Aspects of Internalization*. New York: International Universities Press.

Spiegelman, J. 1996. *Psychotherapy as a Mutual Process*. Tempe: New Falcon.

Stern, D. 1985. *The Interpersonal World of the Infant*. New York: Basic Books.

Storr, A. 1973. *C.G. Jung*. New York: Viking.

Tarnas, R. 1993. *The Passion of the Western Mind*. New York: Ballantine Books.

von Franz, M. 1980. *On Divination and Synchronicity*. Toronto: University of Toronto Press.

————. 1992. *Psyche and Matter*. Boston: Shambhala.

Wilhelm, H. 1973. *Eight Lectures on the 'I Ching'*. Princeton: Princeton University Press.

Wilson, C. 1984. *C.G. Jung: Lord of the Underworld*. Wellingborough: Aquarium Press.

Winnicott, D. 1974. *Playing and Reality*. London: Penguin.

4

Epilogue: A Discussion of Synchronicity and Related Matters

I include the following discussion to give the pot a final stir. For many pages now I've been expressing my views without stint and without opposition. How nice it is to have everything my way. However, as I have asserted from the beginning, my aim is not to refute Jung's theory of synchronicity but to offer an alternative to it. In the spirit of that aim, I proffer the material to come. The reader will have a chance to look at both sides of the issue, at least in a preliminary way, and to consider his own position, his own theoretical orientation. Few problems tease the mind as does synchronicity. Whether or not we should *thank* Jung for that, well, who knows?

* * *

I was referred to Dr. Lynne Walter, Jungian psychotherapist and lecturer, by the C.G. Jung Society of Vancouver. Dr. Walter greeted me quietly but cordially when I arrived at the door of her apartment. Entering into the living room with its massive wooden bookcases and gleaming hardwood floors, I admired the view of the Vancouver skyline, the harbor, and the soaring, snow-covered mountains of the Coastal Range. I turned to Dr. Walter. She was a petite woman of perhaps 60 years, with close-cropped auburn hair, small, smooth, rounded features, and deep-set, striking blue eyes. Attired in a tan, full-sleeved blouse, soft, light-green cotton slacks, and sandals, she offered me a cushiony armchair, chose one for herself, and looked over at me with subdued, friendly expectation. I knew from her expression, from her manner, from her "air" as it were, that this was a cultured, educated, fully developed woman, and that I was fortunate to find myself in her presence.[1]

MF: I think of synchronicity in two senses, one soft, one hard. By soft synchronicity I mean simply the correspondence of an external event with an internal aim or issue. One is pondering whether or not to join the local choir when a chorister telephones to extend an invitation. Fate, it seems, wants one to sing. Hard synchronicity I associate with Jung, and with those who influenced Jung: Schopenhauer, Leibniz, Albertus Magnus, Hippocrates, and others. It suggests the universe is *disposed* to trigger synchronicities by virtue of its formal or integrative tendencies. The most famous example, of course, occurs in Jung's office, when the beetle appears.

LW: Soft synchronicity, as you call it, is too open, too obvious, to require discussion. I don't even think of it as synchronicity in any genuine sense. As for your hard synchronicity, I've never felt the need to acknowledge or repudiate formalism when discussing synchronistic events. Jung was a formalist, or better a Platonist, all his life. He came to see things that way very early on, and he never wavered in his view. It's not something that can be proved or disproved.

MF: Do you regard Platonism as a *religious* outlook? Does it fill a religious longing, or need?

LW: In some cases, perhaps. But one can come to this philosophically, after a lengthy consideration of the issue, and make it a fully conscious, reasoned position. To me, it just isn't that important. Synchronicity is a matter of *affect*, of deep, genuine *feeling*, of strong emotion breaking through to the surface to clarify or illuminate something of significance to the self. It is a kind of dawning, a wake-up call to look into the heart of a problem or preoccupation or urge. If you run into your ex-wife around a corner and if it rocks you to the core–if it makes you understand that you still care more than you're willing to admit, you're in the neighborhood of synchronicity. As Jung says, synchronicity constellates the *archetype*, the deep, *collective* level of life. That's where synchronicity comes from.

MF: Why archetype? Why collective? Can't this strong emotion simply emanate from one's past experience? One has repressed or denied his feelings. Then they emerge, and one is rocked by them. Why do we have to bring archetypes in, or the collective unconscious, which is, I presume, what you mean by "collective level"?

LW: We bring the archetypal and the collective in because we can't separate the personal event from the archetypal background. The archetype *shapes* the personal event. What is attributable to the genetic endowment, to the DNA, and what isn't? It's a mystery. We're not monads. We're in the universe. We are interested not only in the individual but in people generally. We want to understand human society, human culture, on a worldwide basis. We all have certain tendencies, certain feelings and inclinations. Jung employs the archetypal perspective because he wants to get at mankind, womankind, the human species. When you look at a dog you see a dog and Dog. When you look at a person you see a person and Human Being. Our insight *grows* as we relate the individual to the collective, in reference to both body and mind.

MF: Most assuredly. But are you not referring merely to the innate or institutional side of human behavior? Are not "archetypes," as you're using the term, simply instincts? What's the difference between the archetypal and the instinctual?

LW: Not a great deal. But remember, "archetype" refers to the early stages of our biological *and our cultural* experience, not just to the biological. "Archetype" allows us to see the *religious* element emerging in relation to instinct. Long ago, as ancient peoples witnessed all the creation and destruction in the world, as they saw the seasons pass, as they watched life come forth and death take life away, they were filled with awe, with a sense of the sacred. They *honored* the world in a particular, spiritual way, and they *expressed* this. The archetype, as opposed to the instinct, allows us to grasp the symbolic creations of people, their religious artistic renderings of the universe that surrounds them. As Jung always maintained, archetypes are close to instincts but they ultimately transcend instincts to characterize us as *people*, as human beings. Archetypes *distinguish* us from the animals. Moreover, the timeless symbols of mankind were *collectively* expressed. I mean, they have a remarkable similarity worldwide in the absence of cross-cultural communication. If one can't *see* all this, if one insists on grounding his outlook only in personal, individual, instinctual, behavioral factors, he is probably an *extrovert*, one who lives his life from the outside in and not from the inside out. Introverts, by contrast, come from the interior. In Jung generally, and in synchronicity in particular, it is the interior that counts. The interior is all that really matters. I suspect you are an extrovert.

MF: It might be a good idea to leave my psyche out of the discussion. It could sidetrack us.

LW: (Laughs) Fine by me. I just wanted to let you know that I was conscious of your projections. We all project. It can't be helped, particularly when we are not thoroughly familiar with a topic, such as Jungian theory and practice. There is no absolute reality, no absolute objectivity about anything. It takes many, many years of study and concentration to thoroughly understand Jung.

MF: I'm inclined myself to see the projective side of things, steeped as I am in psychoanalysis, and in postmodern thought. But let me ask you this: does not Jung project too? Are not his writings, including those on synchronicity, predicated by his own unconscious projections?

LW: Once you reach the level of consciousness, once you look closely into yourself through what Jung called active imagination, your projections can lessen, or even stop, at least for much of the time. Jung attained this level through arduous, self-exploratory work. He attained what we call individuation. He went about as far as a human being can be expected to go. Don't misunderstand me. I'm not saying that Jung looked at everything, or that he *knew* everything. When it came to infancy and childhood, for example, he didn't pay very much direct attention. There is very little on this subject in Jung's writings. Consequently, we have to turn to Freud and his followers to make up for this hiatus in Jung's thought. But in contrast to Freud and the other therapeutic schools, Jung looks at the problem of *meaning*, concentrates on *meaning*, addresses the issue of *meaning* in the modern world. For Jung, what mattered most of all was the extent to which a person felt meaning in his life, the extent to which a person connected richly and meaningfully to the world around him, *lived* in the full, rich sense of the word. This is, of course, where synchronicity comes in. Synchronicity enhances *meaning*. It enriches one emotionally, affectively, as a feeling person in touch with his real interior. That is why we *believe* in synchronicity, in the *experiencing* of it. It isn't an intellectual or theoretical matter. It *happens*, and it guides a person to insight and knowledge of the self. When you *experience* synchronicity you *know* something, fully, deeply, undeniably. Synchronicity is real because it *works*.

MF: But TV evangelism also "works," does it not? Isn't it "real" when you press your palm to the TV screen and find salvation?

LW: No. TV evangelism is not real. It may give a person a temporary feeling of security or salvation or grace, but it is ultimately a shallow and momentary measure, a kind of ruse. Synchronicity goes much deeper than this. As I say, it reaches down to the archetypal level and touches the collective or instinctual past. Once an individual sees the synchronistic meaning in an event he undergoes a genuine, psychic alteration. It may not be *permanent change*, but it can be the *beginning* of permanent change. Remember, synchronicity as a concept derives from a lifetime of thought on Jung's part. It is supported by a great many individuals other than Jung. I am thinking of Dr. Rhine and his ESP studies at Duke University, and of the great physicist, Pauli, who looked into synchronicity and saw its validity.

MF: Well, from what I know, Rhine's experiments were ultimately a disappointment to Jung, but let me ask you this: do you personally believe that synchronicity is a physically determined, probabilistic occurrence rooted in nature's laws, in nature's way of working, as Jung apparently did?

LW: I think of synchronicity as a *process*, as a complex happening with a *history*. We must not concentrate entirely on discreet events. Synchronicities can occur across time, even across years. May I tell you a story?

MF: By all means.

LW: I met my husband, Steve, at the National Library in Ottawa where both of us were working during the 1970's. He had been born in Chicago, came to Canada in the midst of the Vietnam conflict, and was well established by the time of our meeting. We were very attracted to each other, but we also had our differences. During the course of our marriage, there were wonderful moments and there were stressful moments too. But we stayed together, through thick and thin as they say. Toward the end of the 1970's I decided to study Jung full-time at the C.G. Jung Institute in Chicago. However, my lack of American citizenship, as well as my financial situation, forced me to commute. Yes, that's right, *commute*. Believe it or not, I took a bus back and forth between Ottawa and Chicago on a regular basis until I was exhausted. In the meantime, my husband had decided to look into the matter of his American citizenship which, for political reasons, was in doubt. In spite of his difficulties with the draft board, he discovered that he was still an American citizen, with all his rights, and with nothing of importance on his record. He immediately sponsored me in the United States. Not only was I able, as his wife, to really get into my studies at the C.G. Jung Institute, and eventually to take my diploma, but I was able to *work*, to support myself, to reside and to *relax* in Illinois. When I told my Jungian supervisor of all this, of my stormy marriage, of my persistence, of my dedication to my new career, and of Steve's ultimate, huge contribution, my supervisor remarked, "isn't it amazing how the snake turns." That's a Jungian expression and refers to the snake as a symbol of life and regeneration, of wisdom in a way. To me, synchronicity is perfectly and unforgettably epitomized in this personal story which I share with you.

MF: Thank you, but with every respect, I don't see synchronicity in this story at all. You've simply described a series of problems and events which were, in the end, resolved because your husband happened to be an American citizen. Again, forgive me, but I just don't get it.

LW: You would feel differently if you could enter into the narration in an imaginative, interiorized way–I mean, feel the process unfolding, the pattern emerging, the river moving toward its natural outlet. There is a *process* involved here, a process that derives from both the conscious and the unconscious mind.

MF: May I change the subject?

LW: Yes, you may.

MF: You recall Jung's beetle, of course. Jung was treating a particularly difficult, stubborn patient who was committed to a rationalistic perspective on the world. She came to him one day for a therapeutic session and narrated her dream of a beetle, an Egyptian scarab in fact. Just at that moment a beetle flew into the office. Jung managed to seize the creature, and then showed it to the patient. The effect, apparently, was electric. She dropped her rationalism and began to undergo a process of spiritual rebirth. You may not agree with every detail of my brief description, but I believe I'm getting at the essentials. We can fine tune as we go. My question is, what are your thoughts on all this as an instance of synchronicity?

LW: I've read Jung's account many times, as you might have guessed. I always think of this episode in Zen Buddhistic terms as a kind of *koan*, a kind of startling, puzzling lesson on the mysterious nature of things. What is the sound of one hand clapping? Such a question can tease the rational mind beyond its ordinary limits. That is what the beetle does. It takes the woman beyond her ordinary, rationalistic outlook. It opens up the world to her as a mysterious, puzzling place that must not be seen strictly in terms of matter and motion. The beetle allows this woman to *see*. She was of course *ready* for the experience. She was loaded with affect, boxed in by her repression and self-alienation. Jung knew this. He knew her well. He had her case history in mind. He knew what she required.

MF: I see the matter rather differently.

LW: How so?

MF: To me, the beetle episode is one of therapeutic manipulation and authoritarianism. Jung takes advantage of his patient. He acts in a psychologically violent manner in order to bring her over to his side, in order to get her to see things his way. Remember, for Jung excessive rationalism is a kind of evil. Jung even calls it "Luciferian" in one place. He claims that things have deteriorated since the Enlightenment [LW interjects that she agrees with this]. He describes his patient's outlook as "Cartesian," referring explicitly to Descartes, the father of the Enlightenment, the originator of the "matter and motion" view. Remember also, Jung writes to Freud in February of 1910 that "religion can be replaced only by religion." This woman has obviously lost her religion, if she ever had any. She's in the hands of the enemy so to speak. When Jung presents her with the beetle, he intends to shock her, to unsettle her, but not simply to get her affect going as you suggest. He wants to give her a *spiritual* experience, to get her to view things in a spiritual or religious way. He sees that as his purpose, as his role as a therapist. "Religion can be replaced only by religion." As the authority in the room, as the authority who is dealing, obviously, with a disturbed patient, Jung exploits his position unfairly. And if there is a negative transference here, as there may well be, it only makes the situation *doubly* explosive. The whole business becomes a kind of brainwashing, a wondrous moment of trickery and tendentiousness designed to flabbergast the patient and to convert her to a religious perspective. Jung has a hidden agenda.

LW: That is nonsense. Of course he shocks his patient. Of course he takes advantage of the opportunity. That's *good*. The woman was blocked, repressed, cut off from herself. Her rationalism was defensive. It kept her from living, feeling, being. Jung's job was to make her live again, flow again, exist again. *That's* his job. Therapy is an *art*, a skill, and releasing emotion is its *goal*. Had Jung failed to take advantage of this marvelous opportunity he would have been remiss. The incident has nothing whatsoever to do with religion, and I believe you are mistaken to think otherwise. Who knows why the beetle flew in? It just happened. It was there. It served Jung's purpose as a therapist. Personally, I do not see this moment as anything other than a remarkable coincidence of which Jung took full advantage. The woman was moved. That's all.

MF: But why does Jung indicate she was moved away from her "Cartesian" outlook, her rationalistic attitude? Why does he write that she was "possessed" by her rationalism?

LW: That was his framework, his way of expressing things, his way of describing her blockage. Jung's aim was always an *emotional* one because emotion is the essence of life, the core of what Jung regarded as *libido*, the flow of living things toward each other and the world, the urge to get in and *participate* in the universe. This woman was on the outside looking in, frozen. Jung used the beetle to *thaw* her. Jung was very different than Freud. He was not preoccupied with words and word associations alone. He was not interested in an intellectual approach to existence. His patient in this case was very probably narcissistic, removed from a living reality by her intellectual defenses. Jung used the synchronicity of the beetle's appearance because synchronicity is of the heart, not of the head, and his patient needed to get in touch with her heart.

Jung viewed each patient individually, determined what each patient uniquely required. He wouldn't have gone ahead with the beetle had he not been certain about the issue. Jung took copious, excellent notes, which are, of course, on file. Eventually, we will be able to see them.

MF: But think of the word "possessed," on the coupling of science and Lucifer in Jung's writings, on the therapist's role as succorer, rescuer, on Jung's insistence that only religion can ultimately fulfill our human longings. Surely you can see that Jung was playing the role of exorcist, striving to remove the Cartesian demons and save the woman's soul.

LW: Not in a Christian sense! That's wrong! Yet perhaps you are not entirely wrong. Jung may have been trying to save the woman's *inner soul*, her spirit, her life or existence in the full signification of the terms. If he is performing an exorcism it is to free the patient up to be a *person*. Religion for Jung meant a sense of the sacred, a feeling for the aliveness and interconnection of everything. It didn't mean some doctrine, some belief, some church. It didn't mean *salvation* as we ordinarily think of it. Jung's religious aims are not incompatible with his therapeutic aims, and not even to be distinguished from them if we view religion in a true, Jungian way. When a person is shut up in rationalism, limited to a scientific attitude, to a mechanical, behavioristic approach to life, he *needs* the salvation of a heartfelt involvement in the world. That's not doctrine, and it is religious only in the *broad* sense of religion, which is *Jung's* sense. This woman was emotionally dead. It was Jung's job to allow her to live once again. She was, after all, *born* alive.

MF: May I explain how I look upon synchronicity? It will take fifteen or twenty minutes.

LW: You surely may. I'm all ears.

MF: [I explain in great detail my psychoanalytic theory of synchronicity to Dr. Walter. I discuss the endless synchronicities of the early period. I go over the theories of Winnicott, Mahler, Stern, Bollas. I describe the internalization of the caregiver, which eventually leads to the individual taking care of himself. I suggest that when a remarkable coincidence occurs it provokes a return of the repressed. The caregiver is once again (unconsciously) projected out into the world. The early period is restored at the deep, emotive level. The individual is affectively, feelingly returned to the time in which the universe *was* watching over one in the form of the good parental object. I declare that my aim is to account for synchronicity on purely naturalistic grounds, to remove from it all suggestions of the supernatural, the paranormal, the divine, the sacred. I close with the statement that synchronicities are *transitional* happenings unconsciously designed to reconnect the individual with the maternal presence of life's early stages. I ask Dr. Walter for her reaction.]

LW: Well, these are original and provocative ideas, to be sure, but I think you are oversimplifying the early period. It is loaded with bad as well as good contents. To be returned to the early period is not necessarily to be returned to something pleasant or nurturing or caregiving or even trustworthy. Have you read Erikson? Even if a person insists on the blissfulness of everything early on, and tries to stay with that, the dark side, or the shit if you'll excuse me, will eventually make itself known. Pollyanna herself will be unable to escape the bad mother, even as she cleaves on the inside to the good mother.

MF: But that's *my* point! I mean, synchronicity is itself an instance of *splitting* the parent into the parent's good and bad aspect. Synchronicity, in other words, is rooted in *idealization*, in the wishful compartmentalizing of things. It strives to put what is essentially an angel out there watching over us because the person who believes in synchronicity has been, as it were, seduced by his infantile desires. The miraculous coincidence triggers his supernatural bent, his appetite for a miraculous and ultimately false view of the world around him. Surely people *do* this. Surely people do put silver linings into clouds, and rather regularly.

LW: Of course they do. And in some instances a synchronicity is nothing more than an exciting, sweet, benign moment. But that is only a small aspect of synchronicity. Eventually such moments will pass and life will return with all its chaos. A person must go further than this, must tackle the problem of his whole existence and learn to spy the synchronistic process therein. Only then may something really benign occur. Your provocative theory does not account sufficiently for the synchronistic *process*.

MF: But the synchronistic moment *is* synchronicity. Such a moment is the only striking, unmistakable witness to synchronicity that we *have*. The beetle incident expresses the very essence of the thing. If we start dwelling on processes and long-term developments synchronicity will simply fade into normative, commonplace behaviors. Synchronicity will no longer have the striking signification Jung gives it. He may be mistaken. Indeed, in my view he is mistaken. But at least he gives us something remarkable to hang on to.

LW: He gives us through the beetle episode what is perhaps the most dramatic kind of synchronicity. But synchronicity is a bigger, deeper phenomenon than that. It is going on all the time, everywhere, all around us. It is life itself in its little details and coincidences, in its remarkable patterns and processes, its tendency to bring things together meaningfully so that we can see the meaning in the world.

MF: But do not other therapies and theories trace these things too?

LW: Yes, but Jungian theory and therapy go deeper than the others. Jungian analysis finds the archetypal stream on which life and the world are carried. It allows us to see and to *feel* the great, magnificent, timeless human drama.

MF: Are we back to archetypes again?

LW: I guess we are.

MF: Well, there's your snake making another circle! I offer you my heartfelt thanks for this wonderful discussion.

* * *

A few days after my visit to Dr. Walter I received a phone call from my friend, Joan Gillespie. She was at work in the Royal Bank. "I have something to tell you," she said. I had the feeling Joan's information was going to be about synchronicity as she knew I was hard at work on the subject. She said,

> Several weeks ago I read an article in the *Financial Post*, then set it aside and forgot about it. Yesterday I realized I needed it, so on my lunch hour I rushed over to the library, fished it out, and photocopied it.

When I got back to my desk at the bank guess what was smack in the middle of it? That's right, a photocopy of the same article! It had been sent down from the investment section shortly after I had left for lunch. Can you believe it?

I asked Joan how she felt when she saw the photocopy. "Sort of spacey, out of the body, floating above the floor," she replied; "the only thing that kept me on the planet was the bank logo in the upper right hand corner of the copy. I could see it wasn't the one I had just stuffed into my purse." I asked if her spacey, out of the body experience was unpleasant. "On the contrary," she answered; "it was wonderful, blissful, marvelous, like the universe was in league with my aims, working on my behalf." I offered the gist of my theory of synchronicity to Joan. I told her that there *was* a time when the world *was* set up to meet her needs, when miraculous coincidences, or synchronicities, were the order of the day. I suggested that, for a brief interval, she had *returned* to that time, was floating in it once again, feeling its uncanny, magical quality. "There may be something to that theory of yours," Joan remarked after a moment. I thought to myself, time will tell. And then, a second later, time may tell.

NOTE

1. Italics and quotation marks are employed in the following dialogue to indicate accentuations. I leave this, ultimately, to the reader's imagination.

Bibliography

Ainsworth, M. 1983. "Patterns of Infant-Mother Attachment." In *Human Development*, ed. D. Magnusson and V. Allen. New York: Academic Press.

Aziz, R. 1990. *C. G. Jung's Psychology of Religion and Synchronicity.* Albany: State University of New York Press.

Bolen, J. 1982. *The Tao of Psychology: Synchronicity and the Self.* San Francisco: Harper and Row.

————. 1985. *Goddesses in Everywoman: A New Psychology of Women.* New York: Harper and Row.

————. 1990. *Gods in Everyman: A New Psychology of Men's Lives and Loves.* New York: Harper and Row.

Bollas, C. 1987. *The Shadow of the Object: Psychoanalysis of the Unthought-Known.* London: Free Association Books.

Charet, F. 1993. *Spiritualism and the Foundation of C. G. Jung's Psychology.* Albany: State University of New York Press.

Combs, A., and Holland, M. 1990. *Synchronicity: Science, Myth, and the Trickster.* New York: Paragon House.

de Mause, L. 1982. *Foundations of Psychohistory.* New York: Creative Roots.

Easlea, B. 1981. *Science and Sexual Repression: Patriarchy's Confrontation with Women and Nature.* London: Weidenfeld and Nicolson.

Edinger, E. 1972. *Ego and Archetype*: *Individuation and the Religious Function of the Psyche.* New York: G. P. Putnam's Sons.

Feibleman, J. 1976. *Understanding Oriental Philosophy.* New York: Horizon Press.

Feinstein, D., and Kripper, S. 1988. *Personal Mythology.* New York: Tarcher.

Freud, S. 1959. *Inhibitions, Symptoms, and Anxiety.* Ed. J. Strachey. New York: Norton.

————. 1971. "The Unconscious." In *Collected Papers*, ed. J. Riviere, vol. 4: 98-136. London: Hogarth.

————. 1974. *The Ego and the Id.* Ed. J. Riviere. London: Hogarth.

Handel, S. 1993. "Mirabile Dictu." In *Proceedings of the Twelfth International Congress for Analytical Psychology*, ed. M. Mattoon. Einsiedeln, Switzerland: Daimon Verlag.

Hartocollis, P. 1974. "Origins of Time." *Psychoanalytic Quarterly*, 43: 243-61.

Horgan, J. 1996. "Why Freud Isn't Dead." *Scientific American*, December: 106-11.

Houston, J. 1996. *A Mythic Life: Learning to Live Our Greater Story*. New York: HarperCollins.

Hughes, E. 1971. *Chinese Philosophy in Classical Times*. London: J. M. Dent.

Jacobi, J. 1959. *Complex, Archetype, Symbol in the Psychology of C. G. Jung*. Princeton: Princeton University Press.

Jung, C. 1967. *Alchemical Studies*. In *Collected Works*, vol. 20. Princeton: Princeton University Press.

———. 1970. *Symbols of Transformation*. In *Collected Works*, vol. 5. Princeton: Princeton University Press.

———. 1970. *Two Essays on Analytical Psychology*. In *Collected Works*, vol. 7. Princeton: Princeton University Press.

———. 1973. *Letters*, vols. 1 and 2. Princeton: Princeton University Press.

———. 1974. *Introduction to the Religious and Psychological Problems of Alchemy*. In *Collected Works*, vol. 12. Princeton: Princeton University Press.

———. 1975. *Aion*. In *Collected Works*, vol. 9, part 2. Princeton: Princeton University Press.

———. 1975. *Civilization in Transition*. In *Collected Works*, vol. 10. Princeton: Princeton University Press.

———. 1976. "The Father in the Destiny of the Individual." In *Freud and Psychoanalysis. Collected Works*, vol. 4. Princeton: Princeton University Press.

———. 1981. *On Synchronicity: An Acausal Connecting Principle*. In *The Structure and Dynamics of the Psyche. Collected Works*, vol. 8. Princeton: Princeton University Press.

———. 1981. *On the Nature of the Psyche*. In *Collected Works*, vol. 12. Princeton: Princeton University Press.

———. 1981. *The Structure and Dynamics of the Psyche*. In *Collected Works*, vol. 8. Princeton: Princeton University Press.

———. 1982. *Psychology and Religion: West and East*. In *Collected Works*, vol. 11. Princeton: Princeton University Press.

———. 1986. "Foreword to the *'I Ching'*." In *Psychology and the East*. London: Routledge and Kegan Paul.

———. 1990. *Archeytpes of the Collective Unconscious*. In *Collected Works*, vol. 9, part 1. Princeton: Princeton University Press.

Kaminer, W. 1996. "The Latest Fashion in Irrationality." *Atlantic Monthly*, July, pp. 103-6.

Koestler, A. 1972. *The Roots of Coincidence*. New York: Random House.

———. 1978. *Janus: A Summing Up*. New York: Random House.

Mahler, M. 1968. *On Human Symbiosis and the Vicissitudes of Individuation*. New York: International Universities Press.

Mahler, M., Pine, F., and Bergman, A. 1975. *The Psychological Birth of the Human Infant*. New York: Basic Books.

Malinowski, B. 1982. "Sorcery as Mimetic Representation." In *Witchcraft and Sorcery*, ed. M. Marwick. London: Penguin.

Mansfield, V. 1995. *Synchronicity, Science, and Soul-Making*. Chicago: Open Court.

McDonald, M. 1996. "Is God a Woman?" *Maclean's Magazine*, April 8, pp. 46-51.

Meier, C. 1986. *Soul and Body: Essays on the Theories of C. G. Jung*. San Francisco: Lapis Press.

Merchant, C. 1980. *The Death of Nature*. New York: Harper and Row.

Mitchell, S. 1988. *Relational Concepts in Psychoanalysis*. Cambridge, Mass.: Harvard University Press.

Neubauer, P. 1985. "Preoedipal Objects and Object Primacy." *Psychoanalytic Study of the Child*, 40: 163-82.

Neumann, E. 1979. *Creative Man*. Princeton: Princeton University Press.

Noll, R. 1994. *The Jung Cult: Origins of a Charismatic Movement*. Princeton: Princeton University Press.

Peat, F. 1987. *Synchronicity: The Bridge Between Matter and Mind*. New York: Bantam Books.

Peck, S. 1988. *The Road Less Traveled*. New York: Simon and Schuster.

Person, E. 1989. *Dreams of Love and Fateful Encounters*. London: Penguin.

Progoff, I. 1973. *Jung, Synchronicity, and Human Destiny: C. G. Jung's Theory of Meaningful Coincidence*. New York: Julian Press.

Redfield, J. 1993. *The Celestine Prophecy: An Adventure*. New York: Warner Books.

Rizzuto, A. 1979. *The Birth of the Living God*. Chicago: University of Chicago Press.

Rogers, R. 1991. *Self and Other: Object Relations in Psychoanalysis and Literature*. New York: New York University Press.

Roheim, G. 1955. *The Origin and Function of Magic*. New York: International Universities Press.

———. 1971. *The Origin and Function of Culture*. New York: Doubleday.

Roland, A. 1988. *In Search of Self in India and Japan*. Princeton: Princeton University Press.

Sagan, E. 1985. *At the Dawn of Tyranny*. New York: Knopf.

Schafer, R. 1968. *Aspects of Internalization*. New York: International Universities Press.

Singer, J. 1972. *Boundaries of the Soul: The Practice of Jung's Psychology*. New York: Viking Press.

Southwood, H. 1973. "The Origin of Self Awareness and Ego Behavior." *International Journal of Psychoanalysis*, 54: 235-39.

Spiegelman, J. 1996. *Psychotherapy as a Mutual Process*. Tempe, Arizona: New Falcon.

Spitz, R. 1965. *The First Year of Life*. New York: International Universities Press.

Stern, D. 1985. *The Interpersonal World of the Infant*. New York: Basic Books.

Storr, A. 1973. *C. G. Jung*. New York: Viking Press.

Tarnas, R. 1993. *The Passion of the Western Mind*. New York: Ballantine Books.

von Franz, M. 1980. *On Divination and Synchronicity*. Toronto: University of Toronto Press.

———. 1992. *Psyche and Matter*. Boston: Shambhala.

Watson, P. 1981. *Twins: An Uncanny Relationship?* New York: Viking Press.

Wilhelm, H. 1973. *Eight Lectures on the 'I Ching.'* Princeton: Princeton University Press.

Wilson, C. 1984. *C. G. Jung: Lord of the Underworld*. Wellingborough: Aquarium Press.

Winnicott, D. 1974. *Playing and Reality*. London: Penguin.

Zuriff, G. 1992. "Theoretical Inference and the New Psychoanalytic Theories of Infancy." *Psychoanalytic Quarterly*, 61: 18-35.

Index

About the Author

M. D. FABER is Professor Emeritus of English at the University of Victoria, Victoria, British Columbia and a psychoanalytic commentator on religion, philosophy, literature, and art.

ISBN 0-275-96374-8

90000>

EAN

9 780275 963743